Happiness Every Day

Safiya Hussain

New Age Publishers UK

Happiness Every Day

Books also by Safiya Hussain:

Three Thousand Miles for a Wish

Foreword

The facts in this book are stated to the best of my knowledge. I do not claim to be an Islamic Scholar or anything else of the sort, and so, if I have made any errors or caused any offence, I apologise in advance and hope to be pardoned.

I have made reference to Prophet Mohammad (pbuh) but have chosen to omit the words 'peace be upon him', which usually follow afterwards, for the readers ease and to preserve the flow of the book. Please include these words when reading if you wish to do so.

Also, please note that all the quotes of Prophet Muhammad (pbuh) are from authentic hadiths but have not been referenced to also preserve the flow of the book.

In the name of Allah, the Most Merciful, the Most Beneficent

Introduction

The moment you opened your eyes as a new-born, your pursuit for happiness began. Your soul began searching for comfort, meaning, peace and joy.

You are not alone in your quest. People before you, and people after you, all over the world, had, and will have, the same desire to just be happy.

Perfect and Eternal Happiness

Before I speak of happiness in every day, I want to first talk to you about perfect and eternal happiness.

Perfect and eternal happiness exist. No war, no hatred, no jealousy, no sadness and no death. That pure, untainted, ecstatic, everlasting joy is out there.

But not in this world.

Perfect and eternal happiness is reserved for the after-life, beyond the skies, in Heaven.

Why? Because God, Allah, did not plan for Heaven to be on Earth. Life on Earth is a test of our love for Allah. Through the rain and shine He gives, through the happiness and sadness He puts in our lives, how faithful and loving do we remain to Allah?

The sooner you realise that perfect happiness does not exist in this world and that there will always be a healthy mixture of happiness and sadness in your life, then the sooner you will be on your way to becoming happier every day.

Happiness Every Day

Despite the inevitable trials and imperfections of our lives, moments of happiness, peace and contentment can easily be found in every day. They may not be eternally lasting moments, as that is the nature of life, but they are moments that can see you through the day into the night with your soul in a tranquil state, regardless of the weather outside.

It is possible to find a moment of happiness in every situation. When death takes your loved one, the thought that you will see them again soon in Paradise will surely put a smile on your face. When imprisoned unjustly by oppressors, the sun merely gleaming through the bars is surely a sign of mercy from Allah. *'Certainly, with every hardship there is ease'* - Quran 94:5.

Happiness deeply depends on how positively you think and act. Scientific research suggests that a person's happiness levels depend on many factors. 50% is dependent on genetics. Surprisingly, only a mere 10-20% depends on life circumstances such as age, wealth, gender, religious affiliation, ethnicity, marital status, health, occupation, family. And the crucial rest, 30-40%, is dependent on how a person thinks and acts.

This book will help you change the way you think and act, day by day, so you become happier in life.

About this Book

I wrote this book because I felt I, myself, needed guidance and structure on how to find happiness right now. Today. Regardless of the current situation I might find myself in.

The truth about happiness has already been laid out by the most brilliant minds in history. Everything important has already been said before. But what I realised is that the teachings in happiness quotes, talks and books, more or less, disappear from the mind soon after reading them. I found that the key is to not just read words and let yourself forget about them the next day, but actually put theories into practice consistently. Words are words and actions are actions.

I needed something that would tell me, in black and white, what to do today in order to capture some moments of happiness. I needed something that would discipline me and give me daily structure. Rules to follow. Step by step. Day by day.

So, with some extensive research over 3 years, I wrote *Happiness Every Day*. For me, and now for you.

This book is here to help you with your everyday happiness. Written from an Islamic angle, it consists of 365 tips that will inject happiness into each day of your year. This book will; push you to take practical steps to find pleasure, teach you the art of positive thinking, uncover your eyes to show you the beauty around you, entice you to be a better person, instil love into your heart for God and, most importantly, serve to remind you of the ultimate purpose of your life.

I haven't necessarily written this book for Muslim readers. I took into consideration emotions and thoughts of all human beings, but I do use Islam as the primary influence in finding happiness and peace. This is because I, personally, do not believe any form of happiness or peace can ever exist without Allah and His blessings. Allah; the Giver and Taker of happiness.

How to Use the Book

This book is very easy to use.

- Start on Day 1 and follow the steps for the day.
- Ideally, have a quick read of the next day's tip the night before so you are prepared for it – especially if it involves an early morning activity for the next day.
- If it is not possible for you to apply a certain tip on a certain day, then pick another from a random part of the book.

- If you can try to apply the more important and easier tips on a regular basis then that would be excellent for you. Do try to repeat tips as often as you can, but be careful not to over-exhaust yourself. Regardless, some of the more important tips are written more than once in the book.
- Once the year is over, start again.

Apply the tips accurately and you will certainly feel happier, more content and more at peace, *insha'Allah* (Allah willing).

Happiness Every Day offers to be your good companion that will stay with you every single day, for the rest of your life on Earth. But not only that, it also offers to help you on your journey to Heaven; the place of eternal happiness.

Finally, I pray. I pray that you find happiness every day, from today onwards. And I pray that you will one day find eternal happiness, in Allah's Heaven. *Ameen.*

Day

1

Ask Allah for happiness

Today, pray for happiness. Ultimately, Allah is the Giver and Taker of happiness. So the first thing to do today, is to close your eyes, raise your hands and ask Allah to bless you with happiness. It's as simple as that. Allah reassures you; '...*indeed I am near. I answer the prayer of every caller (silent or audible) when he calls upon Me ...*' - Quran 2:186. Your whole life can change with the power of du'aa (prayer); '*du'aa is the most potent weapon of a believer, it can change fate while no action of ours ever can*' - Prophet Muhammad (pbuh). Ask Allah sincerely to give you happiness whenever it is best for you and have complete belief that only He can give you happiness, as nothing is impossible for Him; '*when He wills anything, His only command is to say "Be!" – and it is* ' - Quran 36:82. Allah guarantees to respond, one way or another; He will either give you happiness immediately, wait for another time, or respond in Heaven – whatever He thinks is best for you. Above all that, Allah will love you and reward you just for asking; '*there is nothing more dear to Allah, than a servant making du'aa to Him*' - Prophet Muhammad (pbuh). So remember to make du'aa for happiness throughout the day; whenever, wherever.

Day
2

Imagine heaven

Think of your final destination; Heaven. Close your eyes and imagine yourself there. Be specific. Visualise: having more beauty than any woman or man on this planet, gliding through the grounds of your magnificent palace, being lost in the joyous embrace of your family and friends that had passed away, flying through the white skies of Paradise, catching shooting stars with your hands, kissing moons with your lips, swimming under waterfalls of honey and in seas of melted chocolate, being waited on by Angels who will bring you fruits, wines and cakes. And, not forgetting the most spell-binding moment; imagine yourself finally meeting Allah, the Greatest. Go as wild as you want with your imagination but even then Prophet Muhammad (pbuh) said that; *'Allah says: "I have prepared for My righteous slaves that which no eye has seen, no ear has heard and it has never crossed the mind of man"'*. Ask Allah to make your daydreams come true; *'…indeed I am near. I answer the prayer of every caller (silent or audible) when he calls upon Me …'*- Quran 2:186, and one day they will be real, *insha'Allah* (Allah willing). Let this be the reason for you to smile today.

Day
3

Go outdoors

Go out somewhere nice today; the countryside, the beach or some other natural scenery. Don't be constricted by the narrowness of your building. Light deprivation will make you feel tired. But stepping outside into the daylight releases brain chemicals, serotonin and dopamine, which will refresh your mind, boost your energy and improve your mood. Allah recommends that you go out and travel; *'say [o Muhammad]: "travel on the Earth..."'* - Quran 6:11. So go. Go walk along that beach and free your soul like the bird that swims and sings in the sky. Go walk through the countryside pondering Allah's creation; glorifying Him. *'...And they think deeply about the creation of the Heavens and the Earth, [saying] "Our Lord! You did not create (all) of this without a purpose, glory be to You"...'* - Quran 3:191.

Day
4

Turn your day into a day of worship

When doing anything today, remind yourself of your purpose in life. *'I have not created jinn and mankind (for any purpose) except to worship Me'* - Quran 51:56. You have been put on Earth only to worship Allah. Everything you do in your day should be for the love of Allah. So today, turn your day into a day of worship to Allah, by continuing your normal lawful tasks, but doing them solely to please Him. Minute by minute. Go to work and make an honest living; Allah loves the righteous and commands us to work to sustain our lives of servitude. Eat a healthy breakfast, lunch and dinner; so that you have enough energy to serve your Lord. Pray all your 5 prayers; Allah loves the submissive. Be nice and loving to all you meet; Allah loves the kind. Go see natural beauty and praise Allah; Allah loves the one who glorifies Him. Thank Allah when you have drank; Allah loves the grateful. Resist sin; Allah loves the good. Beg Allah to forgive you when you make mistakes; Allah loves the one who repents. Raise your hands and ask Allah for whatever you wish for right now; Allah loves the one who asks. Throw out all your sadness, worries and fears, by being patient and trusting Allah completely, to eternally take care of you and all you love; Allah loves the one who is patient and trusts Him. Remember Allah at all times; Allah loves those that remember Him. And sleep well tonight; so you are recharged to worship Him again tomorrow. Focussing on your life's purpose will take your mind off unrelated problems, increase your love for Allah and Allah's love for you, and open up the doors of Heaven. This is true peace.

Day
5

Note your positive moment of the last day

Write down one positive thing that has happened to you in the last 24 hours. It might be the fun you had last night with your family during dinner? Go into as much detail as you can – noting the jokes, the banter, the food, the company – so your brain recreates the moment and brings back those happy feelings you had. Re-read what you write throughout the day for an instant boost. Also, please Allah by thanking Him for this moment of happiness and, *insha'Allah* (Allah willing), you will have another good moment tomorrow; *'...if you are grateful, I will certainly grant you more [favours]...'* - Quran 14:7.

Day
6

Sleep well

Make sure you get 8 hours of sleep tonight, no matter what. Say no to going out, resist the temptation to watch a late TV programme and turn off that phone. Sleep is one of the most important factors to happiness, yet it is very easily overlooked. Your mind and body need enough sleep. Sleep provides the necessary energy for the day, which in turn will make you more energetic, pray better, socialise more and generally be more upbeat, which will ultimately lead to increased happiness. Studies suggest that an extra hour of sleep a day would do more for a person's happiness than a $60,000 raise in annual salary. Realise how important sleep is, and it is a great gift from Allah too, so by accepting it, your sleep becomes a form of worship. *'And remember when He made slumber fall upon you as a means of serenity from Him'* - Quran 8:11.

Day
7

Give someone a flower

Go to your garden, the park, or a flower shop and pick out a flower. Give it to your wife, brother, mother or friend. A gesture of love to the lucky person and, if done to please Allah too, a gesture of worship to Allah; both of which will give you happiness and reward. *'Is there any reward for good, other than good?'* - Quran 55:60.

Day
8

Notice Allah's signs in your day

Notice Allah's signs as you go through your day. Every single thing that you experience today – the wonderful dream you wake up from, the nice message you receive from your friend, the dreaded grocery chores of the day, the refreshing walk you take along the river, that scrumptious chicken dinner you prepare and eat, the stars you see at night – all of it, has been put into your day for only one reason. And that is to show you and remind you of Allah. *'Verily! In the creation of the Heavens and the Earth, and in the alternation of night and day, there are indeed signs for those who have intelligence'* - Quran 3:190; *'…"Our Lord! You did not create (all) of this without a purpose, glory be to You"…'* - Quran 3:191. To show you the greatness, kindness and power of your Creator, so that you may come to love Him and fulfil your purpose. *'I have not created jinn and mankind (for any purpose) except to worship Me'* - Quran 51:56. Take a fresh, spiritual perspective of your life, by making note of your given signs today and telling yourself how they remind you of Allah.

Day
9

Exercise

Do some sort of exercise today. Force yourself to get up and go for a run in the park, try aerobics in your bedroom or run up and down the stairs for 30 minutes. Scientific research states that exercise is one of the most important factors in making us feel happy. Certain chemicals, like endorphins, increase drastically after a workout, which results in giving you a happy feeling. And generally, people who exercise are healthier, look trimmer, think more clearly and sleep better. Prophet Muhammad (pbuh) also advised us to look after our bodies, which are a gift from Allah, by implementing exercise into our lives. *'Then which of your Lord's favours will you deny?'* - Quran 55:13.

Day
10

You are richer than billions

Think about how rich you are. You are richer today, not just more than millions in the world, but more than the billions that came before you. Look around you and spot all the luxuries that were not around centuries ago, even for kings and queens. Many years ago there was no hot running water, no technology, no cars, no holidays abroad, no phones, no soft luxurious beds, no cultured foods, no microwaves, no TV, no internet. Yet you have it all in this moment in time. How rich are you! Richer than the kings and queens that have passed. *'Then which of your Lord's favours will you deny?'* - Quran 55:13. Is there really anything to complain about? Say a massive *alhamdulillah* (all praise and thanks be to Allah) for each luxury you notice today, and for existing in a year of relative ease. *'So take what I have given you and be of the grateful ones'* - Quran 7:144.

Day
11

Smile lots

Smile lots today, even if you don't feel like it. Remarkably, by physically smiling, positive signals and thoughts are sent to your brain and it becomes very difficult to breed negative thoughts. If your face is smiling then eventually your heart will smile too. At the same time, smiling at others will brighten up their day and, most importantly, will also please Allah. *'Do not think little of any good deed, even if it is just greeting your brother with a cheerful smile'*; and, *'to smile in the face of your brother is charity given on your behalf'* - Prophet Muhammad (pbuh).

Day
12

Write everything you are grateful for

Today at least, if not every day, write down in a journal, all the things you are grateful for. This could be; your ability to walk to work, the love of your family, the variety of clothes in your wardrobe, your cosy home, your favourite coffee cup or the fact that you live without the daily fear of being harmed by others. Grateful people are happier people, and less prone to stress and depression. Also take a moment to thank Allah for all these things He has given you – He will be pleased with you and bless you even more. '...*If you are grateful, I will certainly grant you more [favours]...*' - Quran 14:7.

Day
13

Control your state of mind

Today, focus on creating a calm and content mind, despite what chaos may be happening on the outside. Bad weather, a recent illness, your annoying partner, rising bills – life on the outside cannot always be controlled, but your state of mind, the most important factor to your happiness, can be controlled. You are the master of your happiness. Realise this. So shift your focus away from impossibly trying to make external life perfect and instead focus on being content within, by seeing the positive side of things, refusing to breed sadness or worry, and maintaining perspective on your life's purpose. *'I have not created jinn and mankind (for any purpose) except to worship Me'* - Quran 51:56.

Day
14

You have the world

You have been given the world if you are safe, healthy and have sustenance for the day. *'He, upon whom morning comes while being safe and sound, healthy in his body, and having the sustenance of his day, seems as if the entire world has been granted for him'* - Prophet Muhammad (pbuh). Think deeply about this throughout the day and recognise the truth of this wise statement from this wise man. You have the world.

Day
15

Give something to the needy

Give, give, give. Give something away to the needy today – perhaps a shirt to the charity shop, dinner to your old neighbour or a small donation to an orphanage. Giving is a key factor to happiness and faith, as making others happy will naturally make you feel happier and also please Allah; both giving comfort to your soul. *'Whoever has extra provision should give from it to the one who has no provision...'* - Prophet Muhammad (pbuh). And don't agonise over the feeling of loss, as Allah will always replace your loss somehow; *'whatever good you spend, He will replace it [with better]....'* - Quran 34:39.

Day
16

Do not worry about money

Do not worry about money today, because your wealth has already been written by Allah. We spend most of our time and energy chasing and worrying about money, yet it is paramount to understand that your allotted wealth in life had already been set by Allah before you were born, just like the date of your death. Nothing you do can increase it or decrease it. So work for your provision in a halal manner, because Allah commands you to work, but don't give your life to chasing and stressing over money, whilst forgetting that the reason why you are commanded to work in the first place is so that you can sustain yourself to fulfil your life's purpose of worshipping Allah (through prayers, spending time with your family, giving to charity and so on). Know that, no matter how much extra time you spend at work when you should be pleasing Allah, how much you stress or how much you partake in illegal money-making acts, the specific amount that is written for you will come to you, regardless. *If the son of Adam ran away from his provision as he runs away from death, then his provision would find him just as death finds him'* - Prophet Muhammad (pbuh). Simply make du'aa to Allah that He puts blessing and barakah in your wealth and focus on the more important things.

Day
17

Trust Allah completely, like the bird does

Train your mind to have complete trust in Allah with today's affairs. *'If you were to rely upon Allah with the reliance He is due, you would be given provision like the birds: They go out hungry in the morning and come back with full bellies in the evening'* - Prophet Muhammad (pbuh). For each of your worries today, let them fall off your shoulders, say aloud "Allah, I trust you", and sincerely believe that Allah will look after you and fulfil your needs of the day, just like He does for the birds. *'…And whoever places his trust in Allah, Allah is Sufficient for him…'* - Quran 65:3.

Day
18

Sadness is a blessing

If you are feeling depressed today, wondering why God, the most Merciful, has chosen sadness for you, then realise that this sadness is a blessing. Allah tells us that we will all be tested; *'most definitely We will test you with some fear and hunger, some loss in goods, lives and the fruits (of your toil)...'* - Quran 2:155. Even His most beloved, Prophet Muhammad (pbuh), was tested with hardships, more than you ever will be. But sometimes Allah puts you through the sad times because He knows that it is when you are at your lowest that you are most likely to; find Him, turn to Him for comfort, realise your purpose in life, know that only Allah is the Giver and Taker, and then submit and be patient with whatever He has willed for you, and perhaps afterwards, be grateful to Him when He makes life better. All this will then ultimately result in you desiring and earning a place in Heaven, *insha'Allah* (Allah willing). *'...But give good news to those who patiently persevere. Those who, when any difficulty befalls them, say: "Surely, to Allah we belong and to Him we shall return." Those are the ones upon whom are blessings and mercy from their Lord and it is those who are rightly guided'* - Quran 2:155-157. The sadness you experience in this life, is actually for your happiness in the afterlife. *'...He will give you [something] better than what was taken from you...'* - Quran 8:70. And remember; *'Allah does not burden a soul more than it can bear'* - Quran 2:286.

Day
19

Note 3 things you are grateful for

Think about 3 things you are grateful for today. That new watch you're wearing? Your husband telling you he loves you this morning? Having healthy eyes to be able to witness the autumn leaves fall off the trees? Write them down on a piece of paper. Re-read and savour these 3 things throughout your day, and each time you do, show gratitude firstly to Allah, and then to those people who play a part in these blessings. Grateful people are happier people, and less prone to stress and depression. Also in Islam, half of inner happiness is to be grateful in good times, an act for which you will also be greatly rewarded by Allah. '...If you are grateful, I will certainly grant you more [favours]...' - Quran 14:7.

Day
20

Learn about stars

Take some time out, perhaps during your lunch hour, to read up on the science behind a star. How do stars differ? How many are there? How long do they exist for? What are they made up of? What benefit do they give you? *'And He has placed the night and the day at your service, the sun and the moon; and the stars are also kept in servitude by His Command. Surely, in this are proofs for people of understanding'* - Quran 16:12. Learning something new and interesting is important for happiness and faith. Novelty broadens your mind beyond the trivialities of daily life, keeps you away from boredom, creates joy when you marvel at life's miracles, and pleases Allah; as He commands us to seek knowledge and reflect; *'and say: My Lord increase me in knowledge'* - Quran 20:114.

Day
21

Be grateful for joy & patient with sadness

Gain some reward from Allah today. If joy comes your way, express gratitude and love to your Lord who gave it, who will then give you more blessings, here or with Heaven. *'...If you are grateful, I will certainly grant you more [favours]...'* - Quran 14:7. If sorrow comes your way, exhibit patience by maintaining firm trust in your Lord's decision and continuing to please Him. He will then reward you with Heaven, *insha'Allah* (Allah willing). *'I have rewarded them this day for their patience and faithfulness: they are indeed the ones that have achieved bliss...'* - Quran 23:111. Realise today that both joy and sorrow are blessings.

Day
22

Ask Allah for what you want in Heaven

Write down 5 things that you dream to have, ask Allah for them, and truly believe that you will have them in Heaven. Do you desire; youth again? To meet Allah? Wonderful children? A perfect man? All the supercars in the world? A physical feeling of constant elation? '... *In Heaven, there will be whatever the heart desires, whatever pleases the eye ....*' - Quran 43:71. Ask Allah for it and you can have it all, and more, *insha'Allah* (Allah willing). '...*Indeed I am near. I answer the prayer of every caller (silent or audible) when he calls upon Me*' - Quran 2:186. Let this be the reason for you to smile today.

Day
23

Attach your heart to only Allah

Focus today, on detaching your heart from your material possessions and from the people around you, and attaching it to only Allah – live life for Allah. Stop chasing wealth and people, and nothing and no one will disappoint you. This world was never created for permanent attachments, as for sure, one day everything will leave you; your family, your friends, your house, your car, your body. Chase Allah. Attach your heart to Him, because; '...*to Allah we belong and to Him we shall return*' - Quran 2:156. Allah will be by your side for eternity. Allah can give you all you need. So everything you do today, do it not for things or people, but for the love of Allah. Living life purely for Allah will turn every action of yours into a form of worship; the fulfilment of your life's purpose. Your connection with Allah will deepen. Your detachment from people and objects will widen. You will not feel hurt or disappointed by people and life in general. Your heart will find security and unwavering peace. Your good deeds will increase. And Heaven's doors will open for you. '*A man came to the Prophet (pbuh) and said: "O Messenger of God, direct me to an act, which if I do, God will love me and people will love me." He said: "Detach yourself from the world, and God will love you. Detach yourself from what is with the people, and the people will love you"*' - Ibn Majah.

Day
24

Success is measured by good deeds

Ask yourself today; 'am I successful?' But do not measure success with fame, wealth, beauty or with the number of friends you have. Those are cheap, manmade requirements. To your Lord, the One that matters, success is measured by your good deeds. How often do you remember Allah, how kind are you to others, how charitable are you, how much do you resist sin, how grateful are you to Him, how patient and trusting are you of His decisions and how much do you really love Him? If you feel that you are not successful, then pile those good deeds high right now. You don't need any tools, financial investment, a PhD, a face lift or wealthy friends. You just need you. Prophet Muhammad (pbuh) was a shepherd, with very little wealth and many enemies, yet he was the best of mankind and most beloved to Allah. Start building on your success today, as the door of Heaven is at the end of it. *'As for those whose scale (of good deeds) are heavy, they will be the successful ones (by entering Paradise)'* - Quran 7:8.

Day
25

Watch the sunrise

Wake up to watch the sunrise – outside your house, in the park or at the beach. The sunrise is one of the greatest natural scenes that Allah blesses us with every day. A magical gift that slowly brings our world out of the darkness and cold, and into the light and warmth – much like life's story of sadness and happiness. To pause and watch this, whilst quietly contemplating life's purpose, will give you a great start to your day, *insha'Allah* (Allah willing). *'It is He who made the sun a shining light…'* - Quran 10:5.

Day
26

Meet a good friend

Invest some time in your good friends. The ones that spread spirituality and knowledge, exude positive vibes and generally express happiness. Call one of these friends today, have a chat, a coffee or dinner. Friendship with good people is one of life's greatest joys. Prophet Muhammad (pbuh) had said that if you have a good companion then his goodness will rub off on you, and having a bad one will mean that his badness will rub off on you. Follow Prophet Muhammad's (pbuh) advice and choose the company of a friend that is good for you; 'a person is on the religion of his companions. Therefore let every one of you carefully consider the company he keeps'. The best friends being; *one whose appearance reminds you of God, and whose speech increases you in knowledge, and whose actions remind you of the Hereafter'.*

Day
27

Accept all that Allah has decided for you

Accept all that Allah has decided for you. Acceptance of Allah's decree is a key factor to inner contentment and true faith. Allah is the Most-wise, He makes the best decisions and His decision-making ability cannot be beaten; so ask Him to do what is best for you, and trust Him. And know that whatever situation you are in right now, and whatever are Allah's reasons behind it, it is ultimately for the best. Whether you have just got divorced or just got married, it is for the best, as you have the perfect opportunity to exhibit either patience in Allah (by maintaining firm trust in your Lord's decision and continuing to please Him) or gratitude to Allah (by thanking Him and continuing to please Him); both of which will open up the doors of Heaven as a reward, *insha'Allah* (Allah willing). *'...And it may be that you dislike a thing which is good for you and that you like a thing which is bad for you. Allah knows but you do not know'* - Quran 2:216; *'...If he (the believer) is granted ease of living, he is thankful; and this is best for him. And if he is afflicted with a hardship, he perseveres; and this is best for him'* - Prophet Muhammad (pbuh). You are exactly where Allah wants you to be, so accept your life; be patient, be grateful.

Day
28

Practice gratitude & patience

First thing in the morning, go to the mirror and talk to yourself. Look yourself in the eye and say: "today, I promise to be grateful by recognising my blessings throughout the day, saying "thank you Allah" often, and showing love to Allah. And, I promise to be patient, when facing difficulty, by trusting Allah to be doing what is best for me, and continuing to please Him." Islamically, for contentment of the heart in this life and the Hereafter, gratitude and patience are the two fundamental attributes needed. *'...If you are grateful, I will certainly grant you more [favours]...'* - Quran 14:7. *'I have rewarded them this day for their patience and faithfulness: they are indeed the ones that have achieved bliss...'* - Quran 23:111.

Day

29

Plan a trip to a museum

Plan a visit to a museum. There should be one near you. Even if you cannot go, transport your imagination into the past and wonder how your life would have been 6,000 years ago. Look around you and think about how different this day would have been, where you would have lived, what your faith might have been like, what kind of job you would have had, how big your family might have been, what food you would have eaten, what clothes you would have worn, what your source of entertainment would have been and how the law would have affected your existence. Ponder over the varieties of life and lifestyles Allah has created over the centuries; *'travel through the Earth and observe how Allah began creation. And then Allah will produce the final creation'* - Quran 29:20. This will be an enriching experience and will, in a positively refreshing way, distract you from your normal daily thoughts, and also cause you to be thankful for modern ease. *'And if you were to count the blessings of Allah, never will you be able to count them'* - Quran 14:34.

Day
30

Expect & act what you want to feel

Today, expect and act what you want to feel. This is crucial. The truth is, that we tend to feel whatever we expect and we tend to feel the way we act. Feelings follow expectation and actions. If you expect happiness in the day and act happy then you will feel happy, as your positive expectations and intentions will make you look out for even the tiniest good moments and filter out the bad ones, and your upbeat actions will lift your mood. If you expect sadness in the day and act sad then you will feel sad, as your negative expectations will automatically make you look out for even the tiniest bad moments and filter out the good ones, and your downbeat actions will drag your mood down. How do you want to feel today? If you want to feel happy today then firstly ask Allah for it – 'Call upon Me; I will respond to you' Quran 40:60 – believe that you will feel happy, expect happy, and act happy; smile at work, laugh at jokes, bring a spring to your steps, sit up at your desk. If you want to feel loved today, then firstly ask Allah, believe you will feel loved, expect love, and act love; say warm words to your partner, make eye contact, hug your friends, hold hands. If you want to feel relaxed today then firstly ask Allah, believe you will feel relaxed, expect relaxation, and act relaxed; breathe slowly, walk calmly, speak slower, take time out. Or more specifically, if you want to have a great time at your friend's dinner party tonight then, ask Allah, believe you will have a great time, expect to have a great time, and act as though you're having a great time when you're there. By changing your expectations and actions into positive ones, the feelings inside you will soon follow the lead.

Day
31

Your heart is a ticking timer

Listen to and feel your heart beat. It almost sounds like a ticking timer. Well, it is. Each beat of your heart is another second passed. The alarm has been set and when it rings that is when your death will arrive. The timer is continually ticking – so know that the seconds of your life are slipping away and every single moment should be a positive one. Today, don't waste time. Start now in fulfilling your purpose in life (*I have not created jinn and mankind (for any purpose) except to worship Me'* - Quran 51:56), by saying and doing only good things that please your Lord – remember Allah, trust Him, pray, be nice to others, smile, give your riches, be thankful, enjoy His bounties, refrain from sin. Look forward to the day you will meet Allah and His Heaven. And if you find yourself dwelling on negative matters, then hold your hand to that timer again to remind yourself. *'The one who remembers death most often and the one who is well-prepared to meet it; these are the wise; honorable in this life and dignified in the Hereafter'* - Prophet Muhammad (pbuh).

Day

32

Drink plenty of water

Drink water, lots of it today. It is proven that dehydration can make you feel fatigued, grumpy, cause headaches and impact on your ability to think. This is especially the case for women. Carry a water bottle with you all day and take frequent sips; it will boost your mood, flush out the toxins in your body and make you look fresher. Take this opportunity to remind yourself of the great significance and blessing of water, and how Allah has made you up mainly of this liquid; '...*and we created every living thing from water*' - Quran 21:30.

Day
33

Love Allah the most

Today, ask yourself; 'who do I love the most?' *'Laa illaha illallah'* means, *'there is no diety worthy of worship except Allah'*. What do you think of the most? And therefore; what is your heart most attached to, what makes you most happy and most sad, what do you rely on most, what would break you if it disappeared? If, throughout the day, you find yourself thinking about your partner, your chores or your business more than you are thinking of your Lord, then, practically, you are making these things your *illah*, the object of your worship. That must change immediately if you are to be a true believer, as your body, your heart belongs to Allah and you were created only to worship Him; *'I have not created jinn and mankind (for any purpose) except to worship Me'* - Quran 51:56. Not only that; Allah is the Greatest and Eternal, therefore make Him your *illah* and He will never disappoint you – unlike people and materials. So continue to love your partner, continue to do your chores, and continue to make a lawful living, but do it primarily because these things please Allah. Make the pleasure of Allah your daily focus and motivation. Practically, what is your *illah*? Say Allah, prove that today and your heart will surely find peace. *'…Those that truly believe, love Allah more than anything else…'* - Quran 2:165.

Day
34

Go for a walk outside

Fresh air is a must today. Sometimes, all you need is fresh air. Rain, wind or shine, take a 30 minute walk outside. Preferably when it is light. Walking will trigger your body's relaxation response, clear your mind, and help reduce stress. Even a short walk will give you an immediate energy boost, improve your mood and of course, keep you fit, *insha'Allah* (Allah willing). So, put your technology away, breathe in the fresh air, and observe your surroundings – from the ground to the sky – pondering Allah's creations. '…*"Our Lord! You did not create (all) of this without a purpose, glory be to You"*…' - Quran 3:191.

Day
35

Wear something nice

Wear something nice today. A bright coloured top, a pretty dress, or a twinkling bracelet you only wear on special occasions. The most important time of your life is right now, as the past has gone and the future may just never come. It is also within Islamic etiquette to be clean, neat and well-dressed. In response to a man's comment about the man wearing nice clothes and shoes, the Prophet Muhammad (pbuh) responded; *'Allah is beautiful and likes beauty'*. Today is special; dress like it is so you feel like it is.

Day
36

Current worries will soon be forgotten

List 5 worries you've had in the past and notice how they don't matter anymore. These worries could have been your first day at school, your final exams, getting into trouble for coming home late one summer, sitting on the biggest rollercoaster at the theme park, finding your first job, moving home, losing someone you love, giving birth, getting attacked on the street. See how Allah carried you through those worries and how they have now disappeared? Allah will carry you through your current worries and they too will soon be long forgotten, *insha'Allah* (Allah willing). So don't waste time worrying about anything today – it's not worth it. Today will pass, just like every other day. *'This worldly life is a trivial [fleeting] gain. Undoubtedly, the Hereafter, is really a place to live'* - Quran 40:39.

Day
37

Do something nice for your parent

Do something sweet for your mother or father today. Take them out for a meal, accompany them on a walk, buy them something, or just call them up and ask them how their day has been. Do this for them, but before that, do it for the pleasure of Allah, as He says that you should honour your parents, speak with them respectfully, *'lower to them the wing of humility, and say: "My Lord! Show them Mercy as they raised me when I was young"'* - Quran 17:24. Allah's pleasure and your parent's pleasure is your pleasure.

Day
38

All you have isn't yours, but a gift from Allah

Today, realise that everything you have in your life is not yours, but is a loaned gift from Allah. Your mother and father, your loving partner, your cute daughter, your 4 bedroom house, your red car, your slender body, your bank account, your eyesight, your favourite cup, those fresh flowers on your dining table; all of it is a loaned gift from Allah and is not yours to keep forever. They are temporary gifts and each gift will, one day, certainly be taken back by Allah – your daughter might die before you, your house might be burned down, you might lose your eyesight as you grow old, you might put weight on, your favourite cup might smash in the sink, or you might just pass away yourself before any of these events can happen. This is the reality. So spend today cherishing and enjoying everything Allah has gifted you with. Be thankful for the gifts. And mentally be prepared to one day, sooner or later, say goodbye to each gift with the contentment and satisfaction that you took only the best from them. *'Surely, to Allah we belong, and to Him we shall return'* - Quran 2:156.

Day
39

Note your positive moment of the last day

Write down one positive thing that has happened to you in the last 24 hours. It might be the joyous moment you shared with your husband or wife? Go into as much detail as you can – noting the laughter, the looks and the words – so your brain recreates the moment and brings back those happy feelings you had. Re-read what you write throughout the day for an instant boost. Also, please Allah by thanking Him for this moment of happiness and, *insha'Allah* (Allah willing), you will have another happy moment tomorrow; *'...if you are grateful, I will certainly grant you more [favours]...'* - Quran 14:7.

Day
40

Be patient with sadness & you'll be rewarded

For whatever is causing you unhappiness, be patient and sincerely trust in Allah today. In Islam, the two fundamentals of faith and contentment are patience and gratitude. Think of something that has been making you feel unhappy, close your eyes and say to Allah; 'Allah, please do what is best for me. I will be patient by trusting You and continuing to love You. I hope You will love and reward me for being patient'. Being patient means that you must not despair, stress and complain, but be calm, accepting and trusting of Allah's decisions, and continue with your love for Him. Note, that Allah is the Most-wise and He makes the best decisions – His decision-making ability cannot be beaten – so trust Him. Whatever the divine reasons for Allah's decisions, understand that your hardship is ultimately best for you as it presents a great opportunity for you to be able to express patience and be granted Paradise as a result of it; *'I have rewarded them this day for their patience and faithfulness: they are indeed the ones that have achieved bliss...'* - Quran 23:111.

Day
41

Remind yourself of your life's purpose

Take two minutes – in the morning, afternoon and evening – to stop, close your eyes, and renew your life's purpose. *'I have not created jinn and mankind (for any purpose) except to worship Me'* - Quran 51:56. Your purpose is to worship Allah, today and every day. You can turn everything you do this day into a form of worship of Allah by doing things with the intention of pleasing Allah – working to provide for your family, cooking and cleaning for your children, smiling at your neighbours, being pleasant to everyone, appreciating His creations, making your prayers, and even sleeping with His name on your lips. It all pleases Him. And if He is pleased, then you will have peace on Earth and eternal happiness in Heaven, *insha'Allah* (Allah willing).

Day
42

No one owes you anything

Realise today that nobody owes you anything and any good that they do give you is a bonus. Unless by law, you have no right over the will of people or Allah. It is important to understand this when you feel disappointed and frustrated by others, or when you try to control the feelings and actions of people to suit you. People are free to be how they want towards you. No one owes you anything. You cannot force your husband or wife to show love towards you or remember your anniversary; he or she has every right not to. You cannot force your friends to be there for you in your times of need, when, for example, your car breaks down; they have every right not to. You cannot force your employer to renew your work contract; he has every right not to. You cannot force Allah to give you happiness during your holidays; He has every right not to. You cannot force your colleague to thank you when you give him a gift; he has every right not to. So do not let these things disappoint you too much, and certainly do not let them frustrate or anger you. You cannot control others and restrict their free will but you can control your reactions, so work on those today by accepting things for what they are and being positive. And if someone does show kindness towards you or if Allah does bless you with something good, then be grateful for it, as it's a bonus. '...*If you are grateful, I will certainly grant you more [favours]...*' - Quran 14:7.

Day
43

Note 10 things you are grateful for

Grab a piece of paper and pen and keep it with you all day. Write down 10 things throughout the day, that you are thankful for. This could be; being able to have a lie-in this morning, your good eyesight, the warm coat on your back on this cold day, the soft seat you sit on at work, the lovely sandwich you have for lunch, being surrounded by your family in the evening, your reliable car, your funny children, your warm home or the nice letter from your friend. Each time you write something, smile about it and say *alhamdulillah* (all praise and thanks be to Allah). Grateful people are happier people, and less prone to stress and depression. Also, in Islam half of inner happiness is to be grateful in good times, an act for which you will also be greatly rewarded by Allah. *'Therefore remember Me. I will remember you. And be grateful to Me and do not be ungrateful'* - Quran 2:152.

Day
44

Light a candle

Light a candle in the evening tonight; when you have dinner, when reading a book or when making your prayers. Watching a candle's flickering flame is like watching snowfall outside the window. Looking at this simple but mesmerising flame will have a soothing effect on your soul, will ease the burdens of stress and has the gentle power to make you more aware of yourself. Even a candle flame is a wonderful blessing from Allah. *'And He has made everything in the Heavens and Earth of service to you. It is all from Him. These are certainly signs [of Allah's powers] for people who reflect'* - Quran 45:13.

Day
45

Eat healthily

Eat 5 pieces of fruit or vegetables today. Blend them to make a smoothie. Juice them up. Make yourself a fruit salad lunch. Or season and roast some vegetables to accompany your dinner tonight. Perhaps you could also buy some vitamin supplements to assist your daily nutrition. There has been scientific research suggesting that eating healthily has a positive influence on your happiness. Also, be healthy to please Allah, as respecting the body Allah gave you and nourishing it with nutritious food is paramount in Islam. *'O mankind, eat of what is lawful and wholesome on the Earth...'* - Quran 2:168.

Day
46

Tell someone about 3 positive moments

At the end of the day, share with your partner, friend or mother, 3 positive things that have happened today. This sharing process is a practice of spotting the good things that happen in the day and showing gratitude for them. As you relive the good moments when telling your stories, your happiness levels will naturally rise. Also, be sure to thank Allah for today's blessings. In Islam, half of contentment is to be grateful in good times, for which you will also be rewarded by Allah. *'Therefore remember Me. I will remember you. And be grateful to Me and do not be ungrateful'* - Quran 2:152.

Day
47

Turn off your electronic devices

For a couple of hours in the evening today, turn off all technological devices – phone, computer, T.V. Use this time to do something of quality; play a board game with your family, have a chat with your partner, perfect your prayers, read a good book or try cooking a new dish. These electronic devices cause hundreds of wasteful distractions and have been proven to increase depression, stress and sleep disorders. Really enjoy your time away from a glaring screen and instead bathe in the simple and natural gifts Allah has given you. *Alhamdulillah* (all praise and thanks be to Allah).

Day
48

Live as though it is your last day

Live today as though you don't expect to be alive tomorrow. *'When the morning comes to you, then do not expect to see the evening, and when you see the night, do not expect to see the morning'* - Prophet Muhammad (pbuh). But that does not mean give up everything and sit on your prayer mat all day, crying. It simply means reminding yourself of your purpose in life – *'I have not created jinn and mankind (for any purpose) except to worship Me'* - Quran 51:56 – and turning your day into a day of worship to Allah, by continuing your normal lawful tasks, but doing them solely to please Allah. Go to work and make an honest living; Allah loves the righteous and commands us to work to sustain our lives of servitude. Eat a healthy breakfast, lunch and dinner; so that you have enough energy to do acts that please your Lord. Pray all your 5 prayers; Allah loves the submissive. Be nice and loving to all you meet; Allah loves the kind. Go see natural beauty and praise Allah; Allah loves the one who glorifies Him. Thank Allah when you have drank; Allah loves the grateful. Resist sin; Allah loves the good. Beg Allah to forgive you for your mistakes; Allah loves the one who repents. Raise your hands and ask Allah for whatever you wish for; Allah loves the one who asks. Throw out all your sadness, worries and fears, by being patient and trusting Allah completely, to eternally take care of you and all you love; Allah loves the one who is patient and trusts Him. Remember Allah at all times; Allah loves those that remember Him. So, if it actually is your last day, then you will not have wasted it away and done your best in serving your purpose and earning a place in Heaven. Find peace in this.

Day
49

Do not speak bad of anyone

Vow not to say a bad word about anyone today. Even when the driver behind you rudely overtakes you, when your colleague speaks to you disrespectfully or when your friend invites you to gossip about her mother-in-law. Say something positive about these people instead, or if you cannot do that, then at least stay silent. Negativity in this respect will bring discontentment to your soul and will also displease Allah. *'Never spy and never backbite one another. Would one of you like to eat the flesh of his dead brother? You would hate it (so hate backbiting). And fear Allah. Verily, Allah is the One who forgives and accepts repentance. Most Merciful'* - Quran 49:12.

Day
50

Give your excess clothes to charity

Today, empty your wardrobe of all the clothes that you have not worn for a year. Having too many material possessions will weigh you down, physically and mentally. Give them to charity. You are removing excess in your life and helping those in need at the same time. Allah gives you wealth only to test your faith; are you selfish or selfless? Excessive spending will have to be accounted for. Prophet Muhammad (pbuh) said: *'the son of Adam will not pass away from Allah until he is asked about five things…'*, the fourth being; *'how did he spend his wealth...'* From now on, try to only buy what you need and share your excess with the needy – this is better for your soul. *'…The righteous is the one who…gives wealth, in spite of love for it, to relatives, orphans, the needy…'* - Quran 2:177.

Day
51

Seek Allah's pleasure

Seek the pleasure of Allah all day today, as He tells us that nothing can make us happier than this. Spend this day praying your salah, uttering good words about Allah, doing nice things for others, thanking Him for blessings, trusting Him during tough moments, and resisting sin – these things please Allah. Allah says in the Quran (9:72) that He has promised the believers; *'gardens under which rivers flow, 'where they shall live forever, and beautiful mansions in Eternal Heaven. But the greatest bliss (happiness) is the Good Pleasure of Allah. That is the ultimate success.'* Feel happy knowing that you are gaining Allah's pleasure.

Day
52

Be like a traveller at a temporary stop

Close your eyes and think about this. You are at a train station stop, waiting for your train to London. You grab a coffee and a sandwich. You make yourself temporarily comfortable, find a nice seat and have a brief chat with your neighbour whilst watching people board trains. But this stop does not matter. You're always checking your watch, looking out for your train and thinking about your final destination; London. This is what life on Earth is; a temporary stop. Planet Earth is the train station, death is the train and the Hereafter is the final destination. Today, *'be in this world as though you are a traveller'*, as Prophet Muhammad (pbuh) had advised – at that train station. Don't make yourself too comfortable here, don't attach yourself to those who you meet, check your watch often today, look out for your train and always think about the Hereafter. Your heart will find peace in this way of life, *insha'Allah* (Allah willing).

Day
53

Spend quality time with someone you love

Take an hour out today to spend quality time with someone who you love at home. Cook dinner with your spouse? Play a board game with your nieces and nephews? Have a coffee and chat with your mother? Really enjoy and savour the company. Allah has created us in such a way that we have a natural human need to be close and intimate with other human beings, so having strong and loving relationships fulfil that need, which in turn give you tranquillity. *'And Allah has made for you from your homes a place of rest'* - Quran 16:80.

Day
54

If you want something, ask Allah

If you want something, ask. Ask Allah for it. Today. It is as simple as that. Allah reassures you; '...*indeed I am near. I answer the prayer of every caller (silent or audible) when he calls upon Me ...*' - Quran 2:186. Your whole life can change with the power of du'aa; '*du'aa is the most potent weapon of a believer, it can change fate while no action of ours ever can*' - Prophet Muhammad (pbuh). Do you want ease from your illness? Peace in your home? A stress-free day? Your boss to be kind to you? Raise your hands, ask Allah for it sincerely, ask that He ultimately does what is best for you in this matter, and have complete belief that only He can give you what you want, as nothing is impossible for Him; '*when He wills anything, His only command is to say "Be!" – and it is*' - Quran 36:82. Allah guarantees to respond, one way or another. If He wills, He will give you what you want immediately, otherwise He will respond another time in another positive form or He will respond in Heaven – whatever He thinks is best for you. And above all that, Allah will love you and reward you just for asking; '*there is nothing more dear to Allah, than a servant making du'aa to Him*' - Prophet Muhammad (pbuh).

Day
55

Write 'A' on your hand for *Alhamdulillah*

Get a pen and write an 'A' on the back of your hand. 'A' for *Alhamdulillah* (all praise and thanks be to Allah). Every time you see that 'A', look around you for something that you have been gifted with by Allah. This could be; a sunny day, a cool drink, a piece of chocolate, a seat on the bus home or a good friend in your company. Each time, smile and say *alhamdulillah*. Grateful people are happier people, and less prone to stress and depression. Also in Islam, half of inner happiness is to be grateful in good times, an act for which you will also be greatly rewarded by Allah. '...*And Allah will soon reward the grateful ones*' - Quran 3:144.

Day
56

Exercise to boost physical & mental energy

Give yourself a physical and mental energy boost this morning by doing some exercise in your house (or you could do your own preferred workout). Stretch first. Then do 100 star jumps, 50 runs up and down the stairs, 100 star jumps again. Repeat if you can. You should be sweating by the end of it and raring to take the day on. Scientific research states that exercise is one of the most important factors in making us feel happy. Certain chemicals, like endorphins, increase drastically after a workout, which results in giving you a happy feeling. And generally, people who exercise are healthier, look trimmer, think more clearly and sleep better. Prophet Muhammad (pbuh) also advised us to look after our bodies, which are a gift from Allah, by implementing exercise into our lives. *'Then which of your Lord's favours will you deny?'* - Quran 55:13.

Day
57

Speak & act positively

Speak positive words and display positive actions today. If someone asks how you are feeling, smile and say 'great', even if you are not feeling good. If you're tired, don't mention it and straighten up. If you're feeling sad, don't display it and act cheerful. The more your negative feelings are expressed, the lower you will feel and the more you will spread negativity to those around you. Pay attention to your words, tone of voice and body language. Above all, for Allah's sake, be patient and be grateful. *'Blessed is the man who speaks good and is triumphant; or keeps silent in the face of evil and is secure'* - Prophet Muhammad (pbuh).

Day
58

Be happy for others, to be happy yourself

Be happy for others, to be happy yourself. When you see someone looking joyful today, driving a nice car, dining with a beautiful family, wearing an expensive necklace, or jetting off on a luxurious holiday, smile and try to genuinely be happy for them from the bottom of your heart. Allah is the best decision-maker, and if He has decided to give great blessings to others, for whatever reasons, then accept it and be happy with His supreme decision. Free your heart from the cancer that is jealousy and your heart will become pure, liberated and content. Find your happiness in your fellow human being's happiness. Above that, a jealousy-free person is pleasing to Allah and for that you will be rewarded, *insha'Allah* (Allah willing). *'He is not a true believer, until he wants for his brother, what he wants for himself'*; *'Avoid jealousy, for it destroys good deeds as fire destroys wood'* - Prophet Muhammad (pbuh).

Day
59

Play a game

Introduce some fun and playfulness into your day. Play a game with your spouse, colleague, friend, children or mother. You could play a board game or have a short game of Truth or Dare, Charades, Guess who or even a game of Hand Slaps – winner gets a prize. These are the simplest joys that Allah offers you in your day to escape from the daily stresses of life. Make the most of this opportunity for a burst of happiness, and let this also be the reason for you to show gratitude to Allah by saying *alhamdulillah* (all praise and thanks be to Allah). *'…If you are grateful, I will certainly grant you more [favours]…'* - Quran 14:7.

Day
60

Focus on your blessings, despite hardships

Notice the ease in your life right now, despite the current hardships. Allah confirms; *'certainly, with every hardship there is ease'* - Quran 94:5. Along with whatever difficulties you are going through right now, there is certainly some good in other aspects of your life. You may have lost your husband, but you still have your children. You may have had a car accident, but you are still able to walk. You may not have a house as big as your friends but you still have shelter from the cold winters. You may be tired of the same old routine with your family, but at least you are not all alone. Focus all thoughts on your blessings today and refuse to give any thoughts to your hardships; *'and if you were to count the blessings of Allah, never will you be able to count them'* - Quran 14:34.

Day
61

Revolve your day around the 5 prayers

Let your day revolve around what it was always meant to revolve around – the worship of Allah, via the 5 daily prayers. Arrange the time you wake up in the morning around Fajar. Have your lunch around Zohar. Schedule your work around Asar. Fix your evening plans around Magrib. And fit dinner before Isha. You were put on this Earth to worship, love and please Allah to the best of your ability. Recognising your purpose will give you contentment, perspective and direction throughout the day. *'I have not created jinn and mankind (for any purpose) except to worship Me'* - Quran 51:56.

Day
62

Note a positive moment of the last 24 hours

Write down one positive thing that has happened to you in the last 24 hours. It might be that bargain pair of shoes you managed to find in the sale? Go into as much detail as you can – what you saved, how they look on you, what you would wear them with – so your brain recreates the moment and brings back those happy feelings you had. Re-read what you write throughout the day for an instant boost. Also, please Allah by thanking Him for this moment of happiness and, *insha'Allah* (Allah willing), you will have another moment tomorrow; *'if you are grateful, I will certainly grant you more [favours]...'* – Quran 14:7.

Day
63

Be inspired by other creatures

Watch a nature programme today. These are readily available online. See how polar bears travel through Antarctica with their baby cubs in search of food. How lions scour sub-Saharan Africa looking for a female to mate with. How monkeys play and bond with each other in the jungles. Or how spiders intricately weave their webs to catch flies. Watching other creature's lives will astound you, broaden your mind and senses of enjoyment to life outside of yours, and put your daily worries into perspective. But above all, realise the magnificence of Allah and that surely He should be glorified day and night because of the wonders He has created for you to see. *'And Allah has created every animal from water: of them there are some that crawl on their bellies; some that walk on two legs; and some that walk on four. Allah creates what He wills for verily Allah has power over all things'* - Quran 24:45.

Day
64

Meditate

Meditate for 10 minutes today. Switch off the lights, light a candle, sit on the floor upright, with your hands on your thighs, palms up. Close your eyes. Take a deep breath. Hold it for 2 seconds then release it. Let your breathing ease into a natural rhythm. Strictly focus on each breath and with each one say "Allah", reminding yourself that the reason your Lord keeps you alive and breathing is so that you may worship Him. If you find your mind drifting away, gently bring it back to focus on your breathing and Allah again. This is a perfect way to step away from the chaos of life, bring perspective and calmness to your mind and reconnect your soul with your Creator. *'Surely, in the remembrance of Allah do hearts find rest'* - Quran 13:28.

Day
65

Appreciate your good characteristics

Think of one characteristic about yourself that you like, and that others appreciate. It could be your sense of humour, your generosity, your sweet smile, your helpfulness or your intelligence. There will certainly be at least one thing that you recognise as a gift from Allah. *'And if you were to count the blessings of Allah, never will you be able to count them'* - Quran 14:34. Remind yourself, throughout the day, of the good characteristic you have picked. Reflecting on your qualities will make you feel good about yourself, which in turn will boost your day.

Day
66

Life has happiness & sadness for a reason

Accept today, that life comes with both happiness and sadness for a reason. *'Certainly, with every hardship there is ease'* - Quran 94:5. You must feel sadness in order to feel happiness. See darkness in order to notice light, feel cold in order to know warmth, feel pain in order to recognise ease. If you were happy all the time, you would think people and Earth are the sources of happiness, you would not know the importance of being grateful to your Creator for happy times and nor would you have a desire to go to Heaven, your rightful home. And if you were sad all the time, you would not learn the importance of being patient with your Creator in sad times, nor would you desire the eternal happiness of Heaven because you will have never known or felt happiness. Allah has elevated you by giving you free will, so you may react as you wish to both states of mind. Being patient in sadness and grateful in happiness are the correct reactions and will both gain you Heaven, *insha'Allah* (Allah willing). *'…If he (the believer) is granted ease of living, he is thankful; and this is best for him. And if he is afflicted with a hardship, he perseveres; and this is best for him'* - Prophet Muhammad (pbuh). So surely, sadness and happiness are great opportunities – embrace them both.

Day
67

Do not compare your life with anyone else's

Do not compare your life with anyone else's. Focussing on your own personal achievements and blessings, instead of comparing yourself to others, leads to contentment. Your friend may have a better car, your sister may be more beautiful than you, your neighbour may have a happier family – such is Allah's will. Allah has given you less than some and more than some for a divine reason. Your life is your individual journey – a test of your patience and gratitude. Allah says in the Quran; *'do not strain your eyes in longing for the splendour that we have given to some groups to enjoy as a test for them. The provision of your Lord is better and more lasting'* - 20: 131. You have a lot more than most anyway, but if you want more, ask Allah and you will get it in Heaven, *insha'Allah* (Allah willing). So don't let the thoughts of comparison even peek into your mind today. Concentrate on your own achievements and blessings only, and follow that with an *alhamdulillah* (all praise and thanks be to Allah).

Day
68

Envisage the end results of your goals

If you are working on something at the moment, envisage and pray to Allah for the perfect end result. An exam you are working on? Envisage the joy when it is all over and pray for great grades. A house renovation? Picture the final look and pray it happens just how you want it. Stressful wedding preparations? Think of the happiness on the actual day and pray it goes well. A crying baby in your arms? Imagine the moment she will be able to hug you and thank you for being her parent, and pray she grows to be happy. Keep these positive images in your mind and continuously pray to Allah throughout the day. Allah will respond to your prayers in one way or another as He says; '...*indeed I am near. I answer the prayer of every caller (silent or audible) when he calls upon Me ...*' - Quran 2:186.

Day
69

Choose happiness with a positive attitude

Remember this important fact at every moment possible today; you can choose happiness by simply having a positive attitude. Put a 'No Entry' sign on all negative thoughts that try to get into your mind; your tiredness, your demanding boss, your boredom, your screaming children, your lack of confidence in your work, your loneliness. Actively stop all these thoughts. Green light every positive thought; the warm breeze on your face, your tasty snack, the smile on your child's lips, that amusing cat on the street. Positivity brings happiness. And importantly, positivity is also a display of gratefulness to Allah, which He loves; *'therefore remember Me. I will remember you. And be grateful to Me and do not be ungrateful'* - Quran 2:152.

Day
70

Look forward to Heaven

Do you know what the best thing you could ever look forward to is? Heaven. *'Say: "Shall I inform you of something better than that [worldly life]? For the righteous are Gardens by their Lord, beneath which rivers flow. There they shall live forever and [have] purified spouses and Allah's pleasure..."'* - Quran 3:15. Meeting Your Creator and living in a place where happiness is perfect and eternal. No pain and suffering, no death, no ill feelings, abundant wealth, fulfilment of every single desire imaginable. Think about this today, imagine being in Heaven, ask Allah to save you a place, and look forward to the day you arrive, *insha'Allah* (Allah willing). *'...Indeed I am near. I answer the prayer of every caller (silent or audible) when he calls upon Me ...'* - Quran 2:186. Let this be the reason for you to smile today.

Day
71

Pin photographs of things you enjoy doing

Take some photographs of things that you enjoy doing and pin them to your desk or wall. This could be; travelling to different countries, cycling along the river, cooking new dishes, swimming, visiting the countryside, reading, eating desserts, or spending time with friends and family. Seeing these pictures on a daily basis will remind you of good times, give you brief moments of pleasure and give you an opportunity to say *alhamdulillah* (all praise and thanks be to Allah). *'And if you were to count the blessings of Allah, never will you be able to count them'* - Quran 14:34.

Day
72

Your body's worth more than gold mountains

Really focus on your body during movements in the day. Think of how your eyes allow you to see the birds in the sky, people's wonderful smiles, blossoming trees and city life. How you are able to control your legs to take you from the bedroom to the kitchen for breakfast. How the joint in your elbow bends in order for you to bring your toast from your hand into your mouth. How this food will turn into energy for you to keep going for the rest of the day. Give thought to the sounds you hear. Your ability to think. And communicate. Where would you be without these assets? Each one is absolutely worth more than a mountain of gold. Are you not lucky? *'Then which of your Lord's favours will you deny?'* - Quran 55:13. Smile and say *alhamdulillah* (all praise and thanks be to Allah).

Day
73

Do things solely for the love of Allah

Think deeply about your intentions as you go about your day. When offering to make someone a cup of tea, let it be because Allah will be pleased at your kindness. When giving someone way at a junction, think about Allah first. When you stop yourself from arguing with your partner, stop for the sake of Allah. When you decide not to complain about the weather, do that because you know He does not like ingratitude. Doing things, good things, for the love of Allah will turn every action of yours into a form of worship; the fulfilment of your life's purpose. Your connection with Allah will deepen. Your good actions will increase. You will not feel hurt when people don't respond to your goodness because to please Allah was your main intention and you got that. The state of your tranquillity will rise. And Heavens doors will open for you. *'Allah will ask on the Day of Judgment: "Where are those who loved each other for the sake of My glory? Today – on a day when there is no shade but mine – I shall shade them with My shade"'* - Prophet Muhammad (pbuh).

Day
74

Imagine you are dead

At any point in the day, lie down for 10 minutes, with your eyes closed and imagine you are dead. Imagine you are in your cold, wet grave. You have left behind your mother, your brother, your daughters, your husband, your best friend, your job, your clothes, your home with the garden, your BMW, your bank account with all your savings. Life has passed and you are all alone. Death is inevitable. It is coming. Remember death often so you will consider your daily worries to be insignificant and rather, you will spend your short time on Earth fulfilling your purpose of pleasing Allah, doing good things, fighting less, cherishing blessings, and striving for a place in Heaven; where there will be eternal bliss. *'The one who remembers death most often and the one who is well-prepared to meet it; these are the wise; honorable in this life and dignified in the Hereafter'* - Prophet Muhammad (pbuh).

Day
75

Write 3 things you are grateful for today

Think about 3 things you are grateful for today. Having such cute little children? Being in a stable job? Having the opportunity to dine out tonight? Write them down on a piece of paper. Re-read and savour these 3 things throughout your day, and each time you do, show gratitude firstly to Allah, and then to those people who play a part in these blessings. Grateful people are happier people, and less prone to stress and depression. Also in Islam, half of inner happiness is to be grateful in good times, an act for which you will also be greatly rewarded by Allah. *'...If you are grateful, I will certainly grant you more [favours]...'* - Quran 14:7.

Day
76

Learn about human birth

Take a few minutes out, during your break, to read up on the science of how a human being is born. Follow the moments that a male sperm meets a female egg, producing an embryo, which then grows into a foetus, slowly shaping into a baby and finally, when ready, is pushed out of the mother's womb. Marvel at the greatest miracle Allah has blessed us with. Expand your mind beyond the trivialities of daily life and enrich it with knowledge you can pass to others for the rest of time. Learning something interesting will bring happiness and self-satisfaction into your day. And such learning will also cause you to reflect on the Greatness of Allah and rightfully praise Him. *'Travel through the Earth and observe how Allah began creation. And then Allah will produce the final creation'* - Quran 29:20.

Day
77

Sleep following the Islamic etiquettes

When you go to sleep tonight, follow the Islamic etiquettes for a blessed nights rest. Sleep in a state of purity (ablution). Lay on your right side. Recite *SubhanAllah* 33 times, *Alhamdulillah* 33 times, and *Allahu akbar* 34 times. And blow over your body. Prophet Muhammad (pbuh) said that doing this will remove fatigue and revitalise a person to such an extent that it is better than having a servant. Also, Allah has made sleep to be a gift for you, so by accepting this gift and remembering Allah before sleeping you are turning your sleep into a form of worship. *'And remember when He made slumber fall upon you as a means of serenity from Him'* - Quran 8:11.

Day
78

Write a gratitude letter to Allah

Write a gratitude letter to Allah. Write down as many of the blessings you have received in the past year that you can think of and detail how you feel about them. A fully functioning body. Intelligence intact. A good job. Residence in a civilised country. Fun friends. Having the latest phone. Your caring parents. A nice home. Your driver's license. The great days out in the sun. Your frequent remembrance of Allah. Being able to keep all your fasts last Ramadan. The beautiful sunsets you were able to witness. The weekend break in Europe. Let's face it, you will not be able to write every blessing down. *'And if you were to count the blessings of Allah, never will you be able to count them'* - Quran 14:34. See how you have much to be smiling about, so smile. And by writing this thank you letter, you will be rewarded. *'...And Allah will soon reward the grateful ones'* - Quran 3: 144.

Day
79

Reject all worries for the future

If you have any worries about the future, such as; getting married, passing your exams, being cured of an illness, finding a decent job, being able to afford a house, having a family, or so on, then stop right now. Do you know what will happen tomorrow? No. Will your agitation help change the future? No. Refuse to breed these thoughts today. Throw them out each time they enter your mind. Know that *'what hit you, could not have missed you and what missed you could not have hit you'*, as said by Prophet Muhammad (pbuh). Destiny is destiny, fate is fate. Know that nothing has happened, or nothing will happen, except what Allah meant to be. Only lawful du'aa can make changes to what is already written; *'du'aa is the most potent weapon of a believer, it can change fate while no action of ours ever can'* - Prophet Muhammad (pbuh). So instead of worrying, raise your hands and ask Allah to do what is best for you, should tomorrow come. *'…Indeed I am near. I answer the prayer of every caller (silent or audible) when he calls upon Me …'* - Quran 2:186. And now really trust Him to do what is best for you and leave it to Him to show you the way. *'…And whoever places his trust in Allah, Allah is Sufficient for him, for Allah will surely accomplish His Purpose: For verily, Allah has appointed for all things a due proportion'* - Quran 65:3.

Day
80

Chase Allah, not the world

Today, stop yourself from chasing money for wealth, fame for respect and people for love. What you chase is temporary and will certainly leave you or disappoint you one day. The true source of wealth, respect and love is Allah. So chase Allah, *al-Khaliq* (the Creator), *al-Wahhab* (the Giver of all), *al-Waddud* (the source of love). Live your day running only after Him and doing things only to please Him; be it by praying your 5 prayers, providing for your family, making your friends smile, appreciating Allah's gifts, giving to charity or speaking good words. *'A man came to the Prophet (pbuh) and said: "O Messenger of God, direct me to an act, which if I do, God will love me and people will love me." He said: "Detach yourself from the world, and God will love you. Detach yourself from what is with the people, and the people will love you"'* - Ibn Majah.

Day
81

Talk to Allah, He is your Friend

Talk to Allah. As you go through your daily thoughts – whilst washing breakfast dishes, eating lunch, driving to work, emailing your customers or running on the treadmill – turn your thoughts into a conversation with Allah. Allah is your Friend and you can chat to Him about anything. As you enjoy your sandwich, say in your mind 'Allah, this is delicious, thank you!' If you are annoyed with your partner, talk to Allah about why and ask Him to turn your feelings into love. Speak to Allah of your joys and sadness. Ask Him to help you, and He will. You will feel so much better knowing that you have this Great, Helpful Friend with you all the time. *'Call upon Me; I will respond to you'* - Quran 40:60

Day
82

Life is full of surprises

Look back at one thing that you would never have imagined would have happened – it might be your partner coming into your life, when only the day before you did not know of his or her existence. It might be you surviving an accident against all odds. Or it might be the great job you now have when your future was once bleak. See how life is full of surprises? It may be that a pleasant surprise will come your way later today. Anything is possible by the will of Allah; *'when He wills anything, His only command is to say "Be!" – and it is'-* Quran 36:82. Hold onto that hope today.

Day
83

Cook a healthy meal

Cook a healthy meal today. Grill your meat, instead of frying. Boil some vegetables and season with salt and pepper. Go easy on the butter and sugar. Eating healthy will make your body feel good, as well as your mind. Respecting the body Allah has gifted you with and nourishing it with nutritious food is also paramount in Islam, so do so for the love of Allah; *'O mankind, eat of what is lawful and wholesome on the Earth...'* - Quran 2:168.

Day 84

Do something nice for 3 people

Do something nice for three people today. Perhaps take your mother for a walk in the park? Tell your colleague her dress is pretty? Buy a chocolate éclair for your friend? But the key is, don't expect gratitude from each of these people. Do these nice, selfless acts purely for Allah's love, because it pleases Him, and your purpose in life is to please Him. *'I have not created jinn and mankind (for any purpose) except to worship Me'* - Quran 51:56. Have no expectation of gratitude and returned favours from people and you will never be disappointed by their ingratitude. Most people are ungrateful to their very Creator and Sustainer, so how can you expect them to be grateful to you? Keep giving selflessly. If you get a smile in return, that is a bonus, but unbreakable peace and happiness lies with pleasing Allah and therein lies your reward. *'We feed you for only Allah's pleasure. We desire no reward, nor thanks from you'* - Quran 76:9.

Day
85

Plan a treat for yourself

Plan to treat yourself today. It could be as simple as planning to indulge in a cup of hot chocolate later on, have a juicy cheese burger for lunch, watch an interesting YouTube clip during your break at work or relax with a candle-lit hot bath tonight. Look forward to the treat and when it arrives, stop to really savour the pleasure it brings. These are the simplest of blessings that Allah has bestowed into your day that can sometimes be taken for granted. *'Then which of your Lord's favours will you deny?'* - Quran 55:13. *Alhamdulillah* (all praise and thanks be to Allah).

Day
86

Make minor decisions quickly

Be decisive! Make today's daily decisions quickly. Of course, some decisions do require deep thought, but don't waste time on non-life changing decisions, like whether to have cereal or toast for breakfast, or whether to buy that coat or save your money, or whether to go out with your friends tonight or whether to stay in and read a book. This is angst that you just do not need. Life is short. Quickly ask Allah to make you choose what is best for you, trust Him, go with your gut instincts and don't look back. Allah makes the final decisions on everything anyway, and accepting this is key to contentment and faith. *'Say: "Nothing shall ever happen to us except what Allah has ordained for us. He is our Mawla (protector)." And in Allah let the believers put their trust'* - Quran 9:51.

Day
87

Plan a trip to the zoo

Plan a trip to the zoo for some time this month. This is a great opportunity to reflect upon and marvel at the various animals that Allah has created; all in pairs – male and female. Such fascination takes you away from the mundaneness of life and brings happiness. Plan it and look forward to it. When you are actually there, remind yourself that every creature you see, is busy in the worship of Allah and be inspired by this; *'do you not see that all within the Heavens and on Earth prostrate to Allah — the sun, the moon, the stars; the hills, the trees, the animals; and a great number of mankind?'* - Quran 22:18.

Day
88

Visit the cemetery & reflect

Visit the cemetery today. Send blessings to the dead, they'll be grateful for it. Also, think about your own death, and how imminent it may be. But don't let that scare you, rather, take benefit from this reminder by; positively detaching your heart from this temporary world, being thankful that today's worries may soon end, remembering the meaning of life – *'I have not created jinn and mankind (for any purpose) except to worship Me'* - Quran 51:56 – taking steps today to live life for the love of Allah, and holding onto the hope of eternal happiness in Heaven. Prophet Muhammad (pbuh) had asked Muslims to visit graveyards for this very reason, as it disenchants a person from this world and reminds them of the next.

Day
89

Notice Allah's signs in your day

Notice Allah's signs as you go through your day. Every single thing that you experience today – the nightmare you wake up from, the cool water you splash on your face, all the people you see in traffic on their way to work, your soup turning cold, the conversation you have with your aunt, the giggles that come from your daughter, your bad mood, the full moon you manage to catch a glimpse of, your tiredness at night – all of it, has been put in your day for only one reason. And that is to show you and remind you of Allah. *'Verily! In the creation of the Heavens and the Earth, and in the alternation of night and day, there are indeed signs for those who have intelligence'* - Quran 3:190; *'…"Our Lord! You did not create (all) of this without a purpose, glory be to You"…'* - Quran 3:191. To show you the greatness, kindness and power of your Creator, so that you may come to love Him and fulfil your purpose; *'I have not created jinn and mankind (for any purpose) except to worship Me'* - Quran 51:56. Take a fresh, spiritual perspective of your life, by making note of your given signs today and telling yourself how they remind you of Allah.

Day
90

Thank Allah for your visible blessings

As often as you can today, pause, scan your surroundings and think of your blessings at that particular moment in time. Your smart leather jacket, your tasty salad lunch, your loving family that asks about your day, the sun shining through your windows, your snoozing baby on your chest. With each thought, thank Allah by saying *alhamdulillah* (all praise and thanks be to Allah). *'Then which of your Lord's favours will you deny?'* - Quran 55:13. Be grateful, and you will feel content. Be grateful, and Allah will be pleased with you and, in turn, will give you more. *'...If you are grateful, I will certainly grant you more [favours]...'* - Quran 14:7.

Day
91

Money does not make you happier

It is a proven fact, that having lots of money does not necessarily make you happier. This is something crucial to understand. Having enough money for decent food, shelter and clothing is an important factor in happiness, and can generally be achieved by hard work. But evidence states that, once you have enough money to support your basic needs, your happiness is not significantly affected by the amount you make on top of that. Having a palace rather than a 2 bed apartment isn't going to make much of a difference to your overall happiness levels, and nor is a Porsche from a Ford Focus. Your optimism and outlook on life is what make a huge difference. *'True enrichment does not come through possessing a lot of wealth, but true enrichment is the enrichment of the soul'*, as re-iterated by the wise man; Prophet Muhammad (pbuh). So seriously think about this golden fact today before you sacrifice family time for work or sit around sulkily, wishing for a bigger house and designer clothes. Rather, spend your time working on the true meaning of life, *'I have not created jinn and mankind (for any purpose) except to worship Me'* - Quran 51:56; be grateful, cherish blessings, be patient, love others, do good deeds and pray. Seek Allah's love and Allah's Paradise.

Day
92

Think of 5 people less fortunate than you

Think about 5 people, who you know well, that are less fortunate than you in some respects. Make a list of reasons you think that they are less fortunate – it may be that they are not with Islam, are not blessed with a loving partner, don't have a mother, are not able to enjoy a walk in the park because of physical incapability or are suffering from heartbreak. This should make you feel grateful for what you have. Grateful people are happier people, and less prone to stress and depression. *'Look at those below you (less fortunate than you), and do not look at those above you, for this is better'* - Prophet Muhammad (pbuh). Also, take a moment to thank Allah for your fortunes; *alhamdulillah* (all praise and thanks be to Allah).

Day
93

Recite surah Yaseen

Recite surah *Yaseen* (Quran, chapter 36) this morning. It is said that by reciting this special chapter of the Quran in the morning it will bring peace and blessings into your whole day, *insha'Allah* (Allah willing). *'Everything has a heart and the heart of the Quran is surah Yaseen, whoever reads surah Yaseen, Allah will write the reward of reading the Quran ten times from him'; 'it takes away from its reader all afflictions and fulfils his needs for the day'* - Prophet Mohammed (pbuh). Place your hope in this today.

Day
94

Fulfil your purpose of the day

Develop an overall sense of peace in your heart today. To attain that peace, you must be satisfied with the way you are fulfilling your life's purpose; of worshipping Allah – *'I have not created jinn and mankind (for any purpose) except to worship Me'* - Quran 51:56. And come to terms with the fact that; *'surely, to Allah we belong, and to Him we shall return'* - Quran 2:156. You are alive today but you will one day die and meet Allah. If you feel you are not fulfilling the purpose of your life well and are afraid of dying then act now to please Him. Make your 5 daily prayers, be grateful to Allah for the good things He's given you, be patient and faithful to Allah despite the hardships, give something to charity, be kind to all those you meet today, love wholeheartedly, and repeatedly ask Allah to forgive you for your past sins, so that you are not afraid of death but rather, look forward to meeting Him and entering Heaven, *insha'Allah* (Allah willing). By the end of the day, you should be satisfied that you have fulfilled your purpose for the day; and this is peace.

Day
95

Have a clear out at home

Pick a room at home and have a clear out. Get rid of clutter; things you have not used in a year, or don't need. Handbags, books, clothes, old electronics, ornaments, paperwork. Give them away to charity or throw them away. Be ruthless. You will not miss this extra baggage. Don't feel that you might need it one day, live for today and trust in Allah for tomorrow. Getting rid of your attachment to material possessions will take away the physical disorder in your life to make space for calmness, freedom and clarity of thinking; help the people you donate to; and lead you to living a simple, non-extravagant life, as Islam advises. *'The son of Adam will not pass away from Allah until he is asked about five things…'*, the fourth being, *'how did he spend his wealth…'* - Prophet Muhammad (pbuh). Our excess wealth is there only to test us – use it for doing good, and from now on try to only buy what you need. *'…The righteous is the one who…gives wealth, in spite of love for it, to relatives, orphans, the needy…'* - Quran 2:177.

Day
96

Keep your final destination in mind

As you walk along any path, there is always a destination. University, work, home, the restaurant, that park bench. Life's final destination is the Hereafter. As you walk today, happily or sadly, to wherever, remember that this walk is eventually leading to death and then to the Hereafter, to Allah. Without a doubt. *'Surely, to Allah we belong, and to Him we shall return'* - Quran 2:156. Keep your final destination in mind today, dismissing all destructive thoughts that may cross your path, and look forward to the day you are walking through the grounds of Heaven, *insha'Allah* (Allah willing).

Day
97

Give yourself some alone time

Give an hour to yourself today. A whole hour to do whatever you want – read, watch TV, have a bath, pamper yourself, pray, go for a walk. Be yourself and be liberated for this hour. Alone time is essential for emotional, spiritual and social health – which in turn leads to greater happiness. Much needed alone time is one of the simplest blessings that Allah has bestowed into your day. Say *alhamdulillah* (all praise and thanks be to Allah) for it. *'Then which of your Lord's favours will you deny?'* - Quran 55:13.

Day
98

Gaze at the stars

Tonight, step outside and look up. Gaze at the stars for at least 15 minutes (weather permitting). Forget about everything else but the wonders of these twinkling beads. You're young again. Make a wish to Allah. Believe that the wish will come true – *'Call upon Me; I will respond to you'* - Quran 40:60 – Believe that there is something greater than you. Be swept away in awe. *'And it is He who ordained the stars for you that you may be guided thereby in the darkness of the land and the sea'* - Quran 6:97.

Day
99

Note your positive moment of the last day

Write down one positive thing that has happened to you in the last 24 hours. It might be the moment you realised you had passed a difficult exam? Go into as much detail as you can, noting the relief and joy, so your brain recreates the moment and brings back those happy feelings you had. Re-read what you write throughout the day for an instant boost. Also, please Allah by thanking Him for this moment of happiness and, *insha'Allah* (Allah willing), you will have another moment tomorrow; *'...if you are grateful, I will certainly grant you more [favours]...'* - Quran 14:7.

Day

100

Write 'B' on your hand, for *Bismillah*

Grab a marker, and write a 'B' at the back of your hand. 'B' for *bismillah* (in the name of Allah). Each time you see the 'B', you will be reminded to say *bismillah* before every activity you begin; putting your clothes on, getting into your car, turning your computer on, making a phone call, picking up your kids or eating dinner. This regular utterance will bring blessing into your activities from Allah, but most importantly, it will remind you, amidst your daily concerns, that your purpose of life is to worship Allah, and therefore everything you do should be in His name, for Him. *'I have not created jinn and mankind (for any purpose) except to worship Me'* - Quran 51:56.

Day
101

Hardships may be good for you

Today, change your perspective on your calamities. When something bad happens to you, realise that it may be for the best. Perhaps you got late for a meeting today, because Allah wanted to save you from a car accident on the motorway. Perhaps you were not meant to marry the man that you really wanted because Allah wanted to save you from the years of heartbreak he might have given you. Perhaps you are not given children because you may not live long enough to be able to take care of them and they would be forced to the streets as orphans. Or perhaps, you are afflicted with a severe illness so that you have the opportunity to be patient with Allah because patience is what will take you to Heaven. '...*And it may be that you dislike a thing which is good for you and that you like a thing which is bad for you. Allah knows but you do not know*' - Quran 2:216. Pray to Allah, that whatever He decides for you, it is for the best, and it will be, as He answers all prayers; '*call upon Me; I will respond to you*' - Quran 40:60. Really trust Him, show patience through your tough moments by keeping your faith in Him strong and continuing to please Him, and this will, *insha'Allah*, take you to eternal happiness. '*I have rewarded them this day for their patience and faithfulness: they are indeed the ones that have achieved bliss...*' - Quran 23:111.

Day
102

Enjoy the world's beauty but Heaven is better

Search for some photos online of the most beautiful natural places in this world, deeply enjoy them, but know that Heaven promises much more. There are much more breath-taking and mysterious things waiting for you above the vast sky. This moment you are in, is an ever so short and distant glimpse of the great moments you are yet to have in your eternal life. Ask Allah to grant you Heaven, and He will, *insha'Allah* (Allah willing). *'...Indeed I am near. I answer the prayer of every caller (silent or audible) when he calls upon Me ...'* - Quran 2:186. Smile, and let the excitement flood in. *'... In Heaven, there will be whatever the heart desires, whatever pleases the eye ...'* - Quran 43:71.

Day
103

Write 3 things you are grateful for today

Think about 3 things you are grateful for today. That warm, soft bed you have just stepped out of? The fact that you had a choice to have whatever breakfast you desired today? The freedom to have a stroll in the park later? Write them down on a piece of paper. Re-read and savour these 3 things throughout your day, and each time you do, show gratitude firstly to Allah, and then to those people who play a part in these blessings. Grateful people are happier people, and less prone to stress and depression. Also in Islam, half of inner happiness is to be grateful in good times, an act for which you will also be greatly rewarded by Allah. *'Therefore remember Me. I will remember you. And be grateful to Me and do not be ungrateful'* - Quran 2:152.

Day
104

Be a slave to only Allah

Be a slave to Allah, and not a slave to people or objects. Really think about this today. Do not let anyone, like your friends and partner, or anything, like money and status, control your thoughts and actions. As Prophet Muhammad (pbuh) advised; everything you do, do it for Allah's love, not for the love of people or for the love of objects. Be kind to your husband for Allah's sake, not for your husband's kindness in return. Dress modestly for Allah's sake, not to show people. Go to work so you can comfortably live and worship Allah, not so you can buy luxuries. *'Say, "Indeed, my prayer, my acts of worship, my life and my death are for Allah, Lord of the worlds"'* - Quran 6:162. This is what Prophet Muhammad's (pbuh) companion, when entering a town to bring people the message of Islam, meant when he said; *'I have come to free you from the servitude of the slave and bring you to the servitude of the Lord of the slave'*. Be free from the shackles of this temporary world – stop chasing after it and it won't be able to disappoint you. Be a slave to your eternal Creator only, chase Him – with Him is where there is no disappointment and where everlasting happiness lies.

Day
105

Sleep for 8 hours

Sleep enough tonight. Ideally 8 hours. Come home early, put that phone down, switch the lights off. Sleep is an extremely simple but crucial factor to enthusiasm for the next day, yet it is very easily overlooked. Your mind and body need enough sleep. Sleep provides the necessary energy for the day, which in turn will make you more energetic, friendlier, pray better and generally be more upbeat, which will ultimately lead to increased happiness. Studies suggest that an extra hour of sleep a day would do more for a person's happiness than a $60,000 raise in annual salary. Allah has gifted us with night in order to rest. Accept that blessing with open arms and by doing so you are turning sleep into a form of worship to Allah. *'It is Allah who has made the night for you to rest...'* - Quran 40:61.

Day
106

Accept all that Allah has decided for you

Accept everything in your life that Allah has decided for you. The size of your house, your past heartbreak, your recent happiness. Know that *'what hit you, could not have missed you and what missed you could not have hit you'*, as said by Prophet Muhammad (pbuh). Destiny is destiny, fate is fate. Know that nothing has happened, or nothing will happen, except what Allah meant to be. No human being or thing can change your blessings or hardships. Only lawful du'aa can make changes to what is already written; *'du'aa is the most potent weapon of a believer, it can change fate while no action of ours ever can'* - Prophet Muhammad (pbuh). Therefore, profusely make du'aa that Allah does what is best for you, and then without fear or regrets, rest your heart with Allah, be patient in bad times, be grateful in good times, and accept His decree as the most-wise and best decision for you. Acceptance of Allah's decisions, by being grateful or patient, is a key factor to inner contentment and true faith. *'Say: "Nothing shall ever happen to us except what Allah has ordained for us. He is our Mawla (protector)" And in Allah let the believers put their trust'* - Quran 9:51. You are exactly where Allah wants you to be, so accept your life; be patient, be grateful.

Day
107

Have a relaxing bath

This evening, run a hot scented bath, light a couple of candles and switch off the lights. Relax, turn off your brain, and let today's stresses escape from your body. This is a simple, yet ever-so blissful gift from Allah. Make use of it and take this as an opportunity to thank Him. *'Then which of your Lord's favours will you deny?'* - Quran 55:13.

Day
108

Be amazed by the life under water

Today, watch a nature programme on life under water. These are readily available online. You will be amazed at the new world that is in existence under water. Whales, dolphins, fish, tadpoles, crabs, corals. Watching other creature's lives will astound you, broaden your mind and senses of enjoyment to life outside of yours, and put your daily worries into perspective. But above all, realise the magnificence of Allah and that surely He should be glorified day and night because of the wonders He has created for you to see. *'And Allah has created every animal from water: of them there are some that crawl on their bellies; some that walk on two legs; and some that walk on four. Allah creates what He wills for verily Allah has power over all things'* - Quran 24:45.

Day
109

Share dinner with your neighbour

Cook a little extra tonight and send some food to your neighbour. An act that is considered to be a very good deed, which will make you and your neighbour feel great, and it will also please Allah. *'Whenever you prepare a broth, put plenty of water in it, and give some to your neighbours and then give them out of this with courtesy'*, said Prophet Muhammad (pbuh).

Day
110

Are you a positive or negative person?

Are you a positive person or a negative person? Happiness can only be found within yourself. Take a look at the way you perceive things today. Do you point out the darkness when you step outside and see the weather, or do you look at the sun escaping through the clouds despite the thundering storm? Do you complain when your dinner is served late, or do you look forward to the delicious meal despite the wait? If you find that you tend to take a negative angle when going through daily matters, then change that. Adopt a positive view to life today by only thinking, speaking and acting positively. '...If you are grateful, I will certainly grant you more [favours]...' - Quran 14:7.

Day
111

Get some exercise

Get into a sweat today by exercising. Force yourself to get up and go for a run in the park, a brisk walk down the road, or a bike ride. Scientific research states that exercise is one of the most important factors in making us feel happy. Certain chemicals, like endorphins, increase drastically after a workout, which results in giving you a happy feeling. And generally, people who exercise are healthier, look trimmer, think more clearly and sleep better. Prophet Muhammad (pbuh) also advised us to look after our bodies, which are a gift from Allah, by implementing exercise into our lives. *'Then which of your Lord's favours will you deny?'* - Quran 55:13.

Day
112

Treat all as if they'll be dead by midnight

Today, treat everyone you meet as if they were going to be dead by
midnight. Be extremely kind and caring to your family, friends,
colleagues, the bus driver, the supermarket assistant. Give them your
time, do favours for them, listen to them intently when they speak,
put a smile on their face and ignore any annoyances. Do this with no
expectation of your goodness being returned by them. They will be
pleased, you will be pleased and most of all, Allah will be pleased;
'...and do good (to others); surely Allah loves the doers of good' - Quran
2:195.

Day
113

Ponder over one of your achievements

Ponder in detail over one of your achievements from the past 5 years. Have you learnt to bake fantastic cakes? Got a first class degree? Passed your driving test? Given birth to a wonderful baby? Started a successful video blog? Lost a lot of weight? Give thought today to the kind of doors this achievement of yours has opened for you or can open up for you in the future. You are worthy and you are accomplished. Feel happy and blessed; *alhamdulillah* (all praise and thanks be to Allah). *'And if you were to count the blessings of Allah, never will you be able to count them'* - Quran 14:34.

Day
114

Have meaningful conversations with someone

Have a deep and meaningful conversation with someone today. Perhaps, discuss the purpose of life? The beliefs of various religions? World poverty? Past wars? Current news? The ups and downs of being a parent? The vastness of the universe? The definition of happiness? The meaning of true love? Research has shown that making less small talk and having more meaningful conversations improves happiness. Especially if it is a conversation that makes you realise the purpose of your life and the greatness of Allah. *'Verily! In the creation of the Heavens and the Earth, and in the alternation of night and day, there are indeed signs for those who have intelligence'* - Quran 3:190.

Day
115

Greet people with a smile & assalamu'alaikum

Give a friend, a family member, a colleague and a stranger one of your smiles today and a greeting of; *assalamu'alaikum* (may peace be upon you). They might be in need of this smile and prayer. And a smile is contagious so yours might make them smile. But don't worry if they don't smile back or respond. Do this as an act of kindness and charity to that person, for the love of Allah. Prophet Muhammad (pbuh) had said; *'do not think little of any good deed, even if it is just greeting your brother with a cheerful smile'* and, *'to smile in the face of your brother is charity given on your behalf'*.

Day
116

Forgive others

Do you have any grudges against anyone? If so, let today be the day that you swallow your pride and sincerely forgive them. And don't look back again. Holding a grudge does you no good whatsoever but rather, burdens you. Forgiveness cleanses the soul and mind of this pointless, heavy, negative and sinful energy. And remember, Prophet Muhammad (pbuh) said that; *'whoever will not show mercy, will not be shown mercy by Allah'*. So let go of the anger immediately, feel free of negativity, show forgiveness and mercy, and Allah will in turn show you forgiveness and mercy. '*...They should rather pardon and overlook. Would you not love Allah to forgive you? Allah is Ever-Forgiving, Most Merciful'* - Quran 24:22.

Day
117

Escape the world through prayer

When you take that first step onto your prayer mat, mentally step away from the world and begin to devote this moment of love to your Creator. In each of your 5 prayers today, for those few minutes, let salah comfort your soul. *'The coolness of my eyes lies in salah'* - Prophet Muhammad (pbuh). Enjoy this peaceful meeting between just you and your Lord. Escape your life and all distracting thoughts, remind yourself of life's purpose and feel sincere love in your heart for Allah with each bow and prostration. For your soul, this is the truest joy. *'Surely, in the remembrance of Allah do hearts find rest'* - Quran 13:28.

Day
118

Contact a good & happy friend

Meet or call a good and happy friend today. It is easy to begin to think negatively when you spend time with people who backbite about colleagues, are ungrateful for the blessings they have, constantly complain about life, use hateful speech towards others, and involve themselves in dark acts. Conversely, if you are around people who are spiritual, positive and happy, their emotional state will rub off onto you. And such friendship is one of life's greatest joys. Follow Prophet Muhammad's (pbuh) advice and carefully choose who you spend time with; *'a person is on the religion of his companions. Therefore let every one of you carefully consider the company he keeps'*. The best friends being; *'one whose appearance reminds you of God, and whose speech increases you in knowledge, and whose actions remind you of the Hereafter'*.

Day
119

Note 3 things you love about yourself

Write down 3 things that you love about yourself – there will certainly be at least 3. Your smile? Your accent? Your humour? Your eyes? Your fitness? Your ambition? Your kindness? Your spirituality? Your skill at being a good mother? Your love of reading? Your ability to appreciate nature? Your cooking talent? Remind yourself of these 3 traits throughout the day. Give yourself a little smile and a "thank you Allah" with each reminder. *'And if you were to count the blessings of Allah, never will you be able to count them'* - Quran 14:34. Learn to love yourself – your happiness begins with you.

Day

120

You are luckier than most in this world

You are incredibly lucky. You have what approximately 80% of the world does not have if you have; a roof over your head, a warm bed to sleep in at night, food and drink whenever you desire, nice clothes on your back, an education to be able to read and speak English, and an opportunity to live a better life. Go about your day today – eating that doughnut, putting your nice shoes on, sitting in your car, going to work, wandering around the park, greeting your happy family, getting into your cosy bed – but with each moment really think about those people currently on this planet who are not able to do what you are currently doing. Say *alhamdulillah* (all praise and thanks be to Allah). *'And if you were to count the blessings of Allah, never will you be able to count them'* - Quran 14:34.

Day

121

Get a plant & observe its life

Buy a plant today to put in the room you spend most of your time in – at home or the office. Spend pleasurable moments getting lost in watching this beautiful life grow before your very eyes, day in, day out. Plants, despite seeming very motionless, are remarkable creations. Just like mankind and animals, plants live and die, they fight amongst each other, compete for mates, reproduce, distribute themselves in new territories and form alliances with certain creatures, but the drama is just a lot slower than that of our lives. Witnessing the life of a plant will intrigue you, and broaden your mind and senses of enjoyment to life outside of yours. It is also scientifically proven that plants in the home or work space can reduce stress, improve well-being and raise productivity. But above all, remind yourself that this plant is in the constant worship of Allah, realise the magnificence of Allah, and that surely, for His creations, He should be glorified day and night just like the plant is glorifying Him. *'And in the Earth are neighbouring tracts of land, orchards of grapes, plantations and date palms, some of which grow in clusters whilst others do not: watered with the same water, yet some of them We make more excellent than others to eat. Behold, verily in these things there are signs for those who understand!'* - Quran 13:4.

Day
122

Put a smile on your face & heart

Put a smile on your face often today, but also put a smile on your heart by doing something good. Perhaps take some bread to the nearest pond and feed the ducks, take some food to the local homeless shelter or call upon a lonely neighbour. This will bring an immediate smile to your heart. And at the same time you have also gained Allah's pleasure in doing a good act. '...*And do good (to others); surely Allah loves the doers of good*' - Quran 2:195.

Day
123

Note a positive moment of the last 24 hours

Write down one positive thing that has happened to you in the last 24 hours. It might be that you have recovered from an illness? Go into as much detail as you can – noting the healthy feelings and what the first thing you did once you felt better – so your brain recreates the moment and brings back those happy feelings you had. Re-read what you write throughout the day for an instant boost. Also, please Allah by thanking Him for this moment of happiness and, *insha'Allah* (Allah willing), you will have another moment tomorrow; '*...if you are grateful, I will certainly grant you more [favours]...*' - Quran 14:7.

Day
124

Ask Allah for all that you hope for today

If you want a good day today – want to feel at peace, want the traffic to not be bad, want a good workout at the gym, want dinner to cook well, or whatever it is – ask Allah. Whatever you find yourself consciously or subconsciously hoping for during the day, directly ask Allah for it. Allah reassures you; *'…indeed I am near. I answer the prayer of every caller (silent or audible) when he calls upon Me …'* - Quran 2:186. Your whole life can change with the power of du'aa; *'du'aa is the most potent weapon of a believer, it can change fate while no action of ours ever can'* - Prophet Muhammad (pbuh). Raise your hands, sincerely ask Allah for what you want, ask that He ultimately does what is best for you in this matter, and have complete belief that only He can give you what you want, as nothing is impossible for Him; *'when He wills anything, His only command is to say "Be!" – and it is'*- Quran 36:82. Allah guarantees to respond, one way or another. If He wills, He will give you what you want immediately, otherwise He will respond another time in another positive form or He will respond in Heaven – whatever He thinks is best for you. And above all that, Allah will love you and reward you for asking; *'there is nothing more dear to Allah, than a servant making du'aa to Him'* - Prophet Muhammad (pbuh).

Day
125

Plant yourself 100 trees in Heaven

Say; '*subhanAllah il azeem wa bi* hamdihi' (glory and praise be to Allah, the Almighty) 100 times today. Each time you say it, it is said Allah plants a palm tree for you in Heaven. A tree so big that it is said it would take a horse 40 years to ride around its shade. Make yourself a magnificent forest! Hold the image of your new trees in your mind throughout the day, with the knowledge that you will one day visit them, *insha'Allah* (Allah willing).

Day
126

Note 5 things you dream to have in Heaven

Write down 5 things that you dream to have, ask Allah for them, and truly believe that you will have them in Heaven. Do you desire; a set of good friends? An endless supply of desserts? A reunion with your family? A house made of diamonds? A life without any sadness? *'... In Heaven, there will be whatever the heart desires, whatever pleases the eye ...'* - Quran 43:71. Ask Allah for it, and you can have it all, and more, *insha'Allah* (Allah willing). *'...Indeed I am near. I answer the prayer of every caller (silent or audible) when he calls upon Me ...'* - Quran 2:186. Let this be the reason for you to smile today.

Day
127

Start chasing a dream today

Think of an old dream you've always wanted to chase or set yourself a new one. Start chasing that dream today. Don't wait for the weekend or the holidays. There is no time like now. Have you always wanted to start a business? Research into your areas of interest and start the process. Do you really want to learn how to swim? Book yourself in for a swimming lesson. Have you a desire to learn a new language? Borrow a language book or start learning some words using the resources online. Have you always wanted to write a book? Sit down with a pen and paper and start plotting. Dreams and ambitions reignite sparks, and instil new enthusiasm and pleasure into life. Say *bismillah* (in the name of Allah), ask Allah for help with your dream, and go chase it. *'You alone do we worship and You alone do we seek for help'* - Quran 1:5.

Day
128

Don't take bad things personally

Don't take the bad things that other people do or say to you personally. The truth is that what people say or do to you is more about them than you. A person's negative reaction to you at a particular moment is dependent on their perspectives on life, moods and feelings of the day, past experiences, upbringing, negative personality or insecurities. One person might think you're amazing, and another may think you're the worst being in the world. That is about them, not you. So if someone is racist towards you in the street, it might be because they have been attacked by a man of your race in the past. If you're partner cheats on you, it might be because of his blatant disregard for fidelity. If your friend does not call you when she promised she would, perhaps she was having a bad day. If you feel your husband does not love you, it may be because of his cold and affectionless upbringing. It's not about you – don't take it personally. Prophet Muhammad (pbuh) said that one of the attributes that will give a person the sweetness of belief is to love another for the sake of Allah alone. So today, don't dwell on people's bad reactions to you. Just love them and be nice to them for the love of Allah. *'Allah will ask on the Day of Judgment: "Where are those who loved each other for the sake of My glory? Today – on a day when there is no shade but mine – I shall shade them with My shade"'* - Prophet Muhammad (pbuh).

Day
129

Understand Allah's words

Read the translation of a passage in the Quran. The Quran is fundamental to any Muslim, yet many Muslims don't understand Arabic. You can either buy a translated Quran from a shop or download one from the internet. Start by reading a short chapter in your language today. These are the direct words of Allah and you will undoubtedly find a stronger connection with Him when you read and understand His book. This will in turn, earn you Allah's pleasure, strengthen your faith and raise your heart's contentment. *'And say: "My Lord! Increase me in knowledge"'* - Quran 20:114; *'surely, in the remembrance of Allah do hearts find rest'* - Quran 13:28.

Day
130

Inspire others with your positivity

Inspire others with your positivity. When in conversation with your friends, colleagues and family, try your best to brighten your words today. If your friend complains about someone bumping into their car, explain how it could've been worse by resulting in an injury, and that gratitude to Allah is in order. If your sister complains about how cold it is today, tell her that it is refreshingly cold and it is great to awaken the senses; *alhamdulillah* (all praise and thanks be to Allah). If your partner asks you how your day was, speak of only the positive aspects and stay quiet about the negative. Throw in a few smiles and compliments too. People will love you for your bright outlook and want to be around you. At the same time, you are spreading good vibes to yourself and others, you are being charitable in a way and you are gaining reward from Allah. *'Blessed is the person who speaks good…'* - Prophet Muhammad (pbuh).

Day
131

Plan a fun day out

Plan today, to do something fun in the next couple of weeks. Perhaps a day out at a theme park with your friends? A mountain climb with the family? A visit to a castle with your spouse? Ice skating with the kids? An evening meal with the girls? Pen the date into your diary. Now you have something to look forward to and something that will boost your spirits whenever you are feeling low. *'Then which of your Lord's favours will you deny?'* - Quran 55:13.

Day
132

Remember Allah & He will remember you

Today, remember Allah as much as you can, and He will remember you. Call out His name when you wake, sing His praises when you see something beautiful, seek His forgiveness when you do something wrong, start tasks in His name, be nice to others for His love, make your prayers with devotion, thank Him when you finish eating. If there is anything you desperately need in life to give you peace and happiness, it is Allah – your Creator, Sustainer and Destroyer. Love Him and He will love you. Please Him and He will please you. '...*Remember Me. I will remember you...*' - Quran 2:152.

Day
133

Do various acts of charity

Be charitable all day today. This does not necessarily mean giving money. Prophet Muhammad (pbuh) said; *'to smile in the company of your brother is charity. To command to do good deeds and to prevent others from doing evil is charity. To guide a person in a place where he cannot get astray is charity. To remove troublesome things like thorns and bones from the road is charity. To pour water from your jug into the jug of your brother is charity. To guide a person with defective vision is charity for you'*. Look out for these opportunities. They are everywhere. For your charitableness, Allah will be pleased with you, people will be pleased with you, and your heart will be pleased.

Day
134

Be patient with 10 imperfections in your day

Grab a piece of paper and pen and keep it with you all day. Write down 10 things throughout the day that are not how you would ideally want them to be, but then actively be patient with them. The long hours at work? Your whining children? That toaster that doesn't work properly? Your inadequate sleep? Your loneliness? Your aching back? Your argumentative partner? Your uncomfortable bed? Your lateness to an appointment? Each time you write something, put on a brave smile, think in what way it could be worse, accept and trust Allah's decisions, and say *alhamdulillah* (all praise and thanks be to Allah). Re-read what you write at regular intervals in the day and practice your patience. According to Islam, half of contentment is to be patient in bad times, by accepting and maintaining firm trust in your Lord's decisions, and continuing to love Him. Above contentment, your patience will gain Allah's pleasure and you will be rewarded with Heaven, *insha'Allah* (Allah willing). *'I have rewarded them this day for their patience and faithfulness: they are indeed the ones that have achieved bliss...'* - Quran 23:111.

Day
135

Write 3 things you are grateful for today

Think about 3 things you are grateful for today. Your freedom? Laying in bed for an extra hour this morning? Not living in a third world country and having to walk a mile in scorching heat for a glass of water? Write them down on a piece of paper. Re-read and savour these 3 things throughout your day, and each time you do, show gratitude firstly to Allah, and then to those people who play a part in these blessings. Grateful people are happier people, and less prone to stress and depression. Also in Islam, half of inner happiness is to be grateful in good times, an act for which you will also be greatly rewarded by Allah. *'Therefore remember Me. I will remember you. And be grateful to Me and do not be ungrateful'* - Quran 2:152.

Day
136

Go out to a natural surrounding

Go out into the countryside, the park or some other natural scenery today. Don't be constricted by the narrowness of your building. Light deprivation will make you feel tired. But stepping outside into the daylight releases brain chemicals, serotonin and dopamine, which will clear your mind, boost your energy and improve your mood. Allah recommends that you go out and travel; *'Say [o Muhammad]: "travel on the Earth..."'* - Quran 6:11. So go. Go walk along that beach and free your soul like the bird that swims and sings in the sky. Go walk through the countryside pondering Allah's creation; glorifying Him. *'And they think deeply about the creation of the Heavens and the Earth, [saying] "Our Lord! You did not create (all) of this without a purpose, glory be to You"...'* - Quran 3:191.

Day
137

Accept all that Allah has decreed for you

Accept what Allah has decreed for you. Allah is the Most-wise and He makes the best decisions – His decision-making ability cannot be beaten – so ask Him to do what is best for you and trust Him. And know that whatever situation you are in right now, and whatever are Allah's reasons behind it, it is ultimately for the best. Whether you have just lost your job or got a new job, it is for the best, as you have the perfect opportunity to exhibit either patience in Allah (by maintaining firm trust in your Lord's decision and continuing to worship Him) or gratitude to Allah (by thanking Him and continuing to worship Him); both of which will open up the doors of Heaven as a reward, *insha'Allah* (Allah willing). '*...And it may be that you dislike a thing which is good for you and that you like a thing which is bad for you. Allah knows but you do not know*' - Quran 2:216. '*...If he (the believer) is granted ease of living, he is thankful; and this is best for him. And if he is afflicted with a hardship, he perseveres; and this is best for him*' - Prophet Muhammad (pbuh). Acceptance of Allah's decree, by being grateful or patient, is a key factor to inner contentment and true faith. You are exactly where Allah wants you to be, so accept your life; be patient, be grateful.

Day
138

Organise your surroundings

Organise and tidy your work space and home as much as you can today. Minimise clutter, put bits and bats away, file papers, hang clothes up, hoover up, wipe surfaces clean, throw out unused items. It is vital to keep your surroundings clutter free, orderly and clean so that your mind feels calm and at peace. *'And Allah has made for you from your homes a place of rest'* - Quran 16:80.

Day
139

Slowdown & concentrate in your prayers

Slowdown in your prayers today and concentrate. *'Do not rush your salah for anything, as you're standing infront of the One who is in control of whatever you are rushing for'* - Unknown. Allah is your Master, your Creator and Destroyer. There is nothing in your life right now that is more important than Him. So take your time in your worship of Him, focus on the words you are reciting and the reasons behind your bows and prostrations, and think of nothing but your love for Allah. For your soul, this is the truest joy.

Day
140

Handwrite a secret note to your loved one

Make your loved one smile today by handwriting a secret note to them. Write on a piece of paper, a sentence or two, to your partner or friend about how lovely you think he or she is. Quietly slip it in their pocket in the morning. Write a note to your mother or father thanking them for something they've done for you recently and stick it on their pillow. You will no doubt be making someone smile today, as well as yourself. And of course, Allah will be pleased with your sweet act. *'Blessed is the person who speaks good…'* - Prophet Muhammad (pbuh).

Day
141

As you eat, imagine being a poor orphan

Every time you eat today, imagine you are a desperately poor orphan who cannot afford the food you are about to eat – an apple pie, a chocolate bar, beef steak, chips, chicken curry, a hot cup of coffee, fresh orange juice. Picture the food you would be eating instead – bread, water, and if you're lucky, porridge. Imagine the hunger you would be feeling. Hold that thought deep within yourself with each morsel you take in today. Appreciate what Allah has given you. You have much to be happy about. *'So take what I have given you and be of the grateful ones'* - Quran 7:144.

Day
142

Give some good advice to someone

Spread your knowledge and give some good advice to others today. You could flick through this book, pick out a tip that you have found useful, and share it with your friends and family. With the intention of doing this to help someone, for the pleasure of Allah, this is one of the simplest forms of charity and worship. Both of which will give you contentment and reward. *'Allah and His angels, and the inhabitants of the Heavens and the Earth, even the ant in its hole, and even the fish, send blessings upon the one who teaches people good things'* - Prophet Muhammad (pbuh).

Day
143

Feed an animal

Give food to an animal today. There should be some non-human creatures within reach; birds, ducks, pigeons, fish, dogs, or even ants. Give them some bread, sugar or left over lunch. Such a charitable act can easily be overlooked, yet it will make you feel good, will give happiness to the animal and will also please Allah. *'You shall be rewarded for kindness to every living thing'* - Prophet Muhammad (pbuh).

Day
144

Zoom in on blessings & zoom out of hardships

Zoom in on and focus on your current blessings – your caring mother, your cosy sofa, your healthy eyes. Zoom out of and don't think about your current hardships. To be grateful for what you have at this moment in time is extremely important in the quest for happiness. No matter what hardships you have, there are thousands of blessings you also currently have; *'certainly, with every hardship there is ease'* - Quran 94:5; *'and if you were to count the blessings of Allah, never will you be able to count them'* - Quran 14:34. Don't believe that only when your hardships go will you finally be happy because that is not true; *'…if the son of Adam has one valley, he will wish that he had a second, and if he had two valleys, he would wish that he had a third. The stomach of the son of Adam will be filled only with dust (i.e. he is never satisfied)…'* Prophet Muhammad (pbuh). Fiercely block all thoughts of your hardships and instead dwell on all the good things in your life at this very moment.

Day
145

Remind yourself of your purpose in life

When things get you down during the day, pause for a minute, close your eyes and remind yourself of your purpose; "I am here to worship Allah". *'I have not created jinn and mankind (for any purpose) except to worship Me'* - Quran 51:56. Focus on just that; doing things solely for the pleasure of Allah – praying, being kind, giving to charity, expressing gratitude, refraining from sin. Anything that is not relevant to your purpose is really not worth stressing over and if you don't give in to worrying then your day will be much more peaceful.

Day
146

Avoid eating too much

When eating breakfast, lunch and dinner today; follow Prophet Muhammad's (pbuh) advice. Let a third of your stomach be filled with food, a third with water, and a third with air. Avoid eating too much as this can make you feel sick, sleepy, lazy, put on weight and is also, not in accordance to Islam. Eat less and you will feel energetic and healthy, and will also be pleasing Allah. *'And eat and drink, but waste not in extravagance, certainly He (Allah) does not like those who waste'* - Quran 7:31.

Day
147

Note a positive moment of the last 24 hours

Write down one positive thing that has happened to you in the last 24 hours. It might be that you found an opportunity to do a good deed that will be rewarded against your name forever. Go into as much detail as you can – what you did and how you felt – so your brain recreates the moment and brings back those happy feelings you had. Re-read what you write throughout the day for an instant boost. Also, please Allah by thanking Him for this moment of happiness and, *insha'Allah* (Allah willing), you will have another moment tomorrow; *'…if you are grateful, I will certainly grant you more [favours]…'* - Quran 14:7.

Day
148

Trust Allah to look after you like the birds

Look up in the sky and watch the birds gracefully roam their territory searching for food. Think about how most of us stress over work and worry about saving up lest we don't have enough money for the next year. Now think deeply about what Prophet Muhammad (pbuh) said; *'if they would only put their trust in Allah as they should, He would provide for them like He provides for the birds who fly out in the morning hungry and return fully satiated'*. Be inspired. Be like the bird. Say "I trust you Allah", and believe He will look after you day by day, just like He looks after the birds, regardless of your changing circumstances.

Day
149

Life on Earth is a temporary pit stop

Remember today, that your time on Earth is merely a temporary pit stop. Life is ultimately a journey from Allah to Allah. *'Surely, to Allah we belong, and to Him we shall return'* - Quran 2:156. Prophet Muhammad (pbuh) said; *'be in this world as though you are a traveller'*. Don't make yourself too comfortable here – this is not home. Don't attach yourself too strongly to people and things in your life – they will soon be gone. Don't dwell on worries, problems and life issues – they too, will soon be gone. Think about the day you will return back to Allah, to home. And always think about the everlasting Hereafter, where you will look back at your years of life on Earth and they will seem like seconds. Find peace in this.

Day
150

Feed a homeless person

Make a sandwich and give it to a local homeless person today or drop some food off at the homeless shelter. Allah will love you for this random act of kindness (which therefore helps fulfil your life's purpose), the recipient will feel happy and your soul will feel comfort. Also take a moment to imagine living a day as a homeless person. How would today differ; what would you eat, what would you wear, what would you do all day, who would be your friends, where would you sleep? Allah has blessed you to be in the position where you have a roof over your head and the means to be the giver of a sandwich rather than the receiver. The roles could easily be reversed. *Alhamdulillah* (all praise and thanks be to Allah). '*And if you were to count the blessings of Allah, never will you be able to count them*' - Quran 14:34.

Day
151

Boost yourself with exercise

Give yourself a physical and mental energy boost this morning by doing 30 minutes of exercise. You can do these exercises in your bedroom (or you could do your own preferred workout). Stretch first. Then do 20 squats, 15 push ups, 15 sit ups, and 20 leg crunches. Repeat as many times as you can within these 30 minutes. You should be sweating by the end of it and raring to take the day on. Scientific research states that exercise is one of the most important factors in making us feel happy. Certain chemicals, like endorphins, increase drastically after a workout, which results in giving you a happy feeling. And generally, people who exercise are healthier, look trimmer, think more clearly and sleep better. Prophet Muhammad (pbuh) also advised us to look after our bodies, which are a gift from Allah, by implementing exercise into our lives. *'Then which of your Lord's favours will you deny?'* - Quran 55:13.

Day
152

Do something you did as a happy child

Today, do something that you used to do when you were a child. Zoom around your living room with toy cars, play hide and seek, have a game of indoor football, ride through the streets on your bike, read your favourite childhood book, have a tea party with your imaginary friend, sit on a swing in the park and go as high as you can. No matter how old you are now, let yourself be that child again so you may relive the simple yet great joys you had when you were young. Perhaps this will inspire you to bring out the fun-child in you in everyday life. Also, reflect on the fact that these were blessings that Allah gave to you when you were young for which you might never have said thank you for. Now is the time to please Him by thanking Him, *alhamdulillah* (all praise and thanks be to Allah). *'And if you were to count the blessings of Allah, never will you be able to count them'* - Quran 14:34.

Day
153

Allah will test you with sadness in life

If you are feeling sad, know that you are not alone and hardships are inevitable in everyone's lives. *'Most definitely We will test you with some fear and hunger, some loss in goods, lives and the fruits (of your toil)...'* - Quran 2:155. Absolutely no one can ever pass life by without Allah testing our faith with various challenges. Even the most beloved of Allah, Prophet Muhammed (pbuh), was tested greatly and even he felt despair at times and cried out; *'when will Allah's help come?'* - Quran 2:214. But, the key is to see this great opportunity Allah is giving you to enter Heaven, simply by exhibiting patience, and then maintaining trust in Him and continuing to please Him. *'...But give good news to those who patiently persevere. Those who, when any difficulty befalls them, say: "Surely, to Allah we belong and to Him we shall return." Those are the ones upon whom are blessings and mercy from their Lord and it is those who are rightly guided'* - Quran 2:155-157.

Day
154

Eat 5 portions of fruit or veg

Eat 5 portions of fruit or vegetables. Blend them to make a smoothie. Juice them up. Make yourself a fruit salad lunch. Or season and roast some vegetables to accompany your dinner tonight. Perhaps you could also buy some vitamin supplements to assist your daily nutrition. Eat healthy, feel healthy. Eat good, feel good. Respecting your body, which Allah has gifted you with, and nourishing it with nutritious food is also paramount in Islam; *'O mankind, eat of what is lawful and wholesome on the Earth...'* - Quran 2:168.

Day
155

Meditate

Meditate for 10 minutes; in the morning, afternoon and evening. Spend those 10 minutes, sat in a quiet corner, with your eyes closed, concentrating on your breathing. Strictly focus on each breath and with each one say "Allah", reminding yourself that the reason that Allah keeps you alive and breathing is so that you may worship Him. If you find your thoughts drifting away, gently bring them back to focus on your breathing and Allah again. This is a perfect way to step away from the chaos of life, bring perspective and calmness to your mind and reconnect your soul with your Creator. *'Surely, in the remembrance of Allah do hearts find rest'* - Quran 13:28.

Day
156

Do something nice for someone

Do something nice for someone today. Say a kind word to a stranger. Share your lunch with a colleague. Give way to a driver. Greet someone with the Islamic greeting, *assalamu'alaikum warahmatullahi wabarakatuh* (may the peace, mercy, and blessings of Allah be with you). Have a coffee with your lonely neighbour. The first person who will benefit from your act of charity is you, yourself. There is a sense of peace and comfort that seeps into the one that gives, there's pleasure in seeing a smile form on the lips of the one who receives, and of course there is a great reward from Allah. *'Whoever does good equal to the weight of an atom (or a small ant), shall see it'* - Quran 99:7.

Day
157

Only Heaven holds true & eternal happiness

Today, begin to lower your expectations of this world. *'This world is a prison for the believer and a paradise for the disbeliever'*, said Prophet Muhammad (pbuh). Our souls came from Allah, and it is only when they return to Him in Heaven, will they find true freedom and peace. If you feel sad today then remember that this world was never intended to be perfect. There will always be sadness, hatred, wars, jealousy, heartbreak, corruption, illness, death and disbelief on this planet. Do not expect a Heavenly life. It is in the Hereafter where your Paradise will be. Have hope in your return to your Creator and return to your true home, *insha'Allah* (Allah willing). *'Oh mankind, indeed you are ever toiling towards your Lord, painfully toiling… But you shall meet Him'* - Quran 84:6.

Day
158

Write all the things you are grateful for

Today at least, if not every day, write down in a journal, all the things you are grateful for. This could be; the soft bed that you wake up in, the nice words your wife says to you in the morning, your car which you drive to work in, the delicious roast lamb you have for dinner. Grateful people are happier people, and less prone to stress and depression. Also take a moment to thank Allah for all these things He has given you. He will be pleased with you and bless you even more; *'…If you are grateful, I will certainly grant you more [favours]…'* - Quran 14:7.

Day
159

There's nothing worthy in life except Allah

Have full belief in the testimony of Islam, the Shahada; *'Laa illaha illallahu muhammadur rasoolullah'* (There is no diety worthy of worship except Allah, and Muhammad (pbuh) is His messenger). Tell yourself today that nothing is worthy of your hopes, fears, tears, independence, love and worship except Allah. So do not let your partner, illness or lack of money be in control of your sadness, tears or fear. They are not worthy. If you want to cry, cry to Allah. If you want to love, love but love for Allah. If you are scared, fear only Allah. Only Allah, the Greatest, is worthy. Having complete, unwavering faith in this simple statement will certainly bring you true success in both worlds, *insha'Allah* (Allah willing). *'...But those that truly believe, love Allah more than anything else...'* - Quran 2:165; *'say, "Indeed, my prayer, my acts of worship, my life and my death are for Allah, Lord of the worlds"'* - Quran 6:162.

Day
160

Gift the world with your smile

Smile at all those you cross today, even if you don't feel like it. Let this be your gift, on this day, to yourself and to the world. By physically smiling, you are instantly releasing positive energy and thoughts to yourself, and to those who see you, which in turn will make you all feel good. At the same time, this is a simple act that pleases Allah. Prophet Muhammad (pbuh) said; *'do not think little of any good deed, even if it is just greeting your brother with a cheerful smile'*, and, *'to smile in the face of your brother is charity given on your behalf'*.

Day
161

Visit the graveyard

Visit the graveyard today and remember death. There is nothing that reminds you more of the reality of life than seeing those who lived just like you, now buried deep in the Earth. Imagine that is you. It will certainly be you one day. Prophet Muhammad (pbuh) advised to remember death often. It will make you realise how the problems you have today are not worth worrying about, and will allow you to renew your purpose in life of worshipping Allah and earning eternal happiness in Heaven. *'The one who remembers death most often and the one who is well-prepared to meet it; these are the wise; honorable in this life and dignified in the Hereafter'* - Prophet Muhammad (pbuh).

Day
162

Learn about the weather

Learn about wind, rain, lightning or thunder by researching online or reading a book on the subject. It is quite surprising that despite the big role weather plays in our lives, the majority of us do not know the science behind it. Allah makes the weather change, but how? How does He initiate the process of rain, in order to nourish the plants which then sustain us? *'Do you not see that Allah makes the clouds move gently, then joins them together, then stacks them in layers? – after which you will see rain falling from between them? Then from the mountainous clouds in the sky, Allah showers down ice, by which He strikes whoever He wills and avert from whoever He wills. The flash of His lightning can almost snatch away eyesight'* - Quran 24:43. Allow fascination and knowledge of Allah's natural wonders to enrich your life and take your mind off daily trivial matters.

Day
163

If you want something, ask Allah for it

If you want something, ask. Ask Allah for it. Today. It is as simple as that. Allah reassures you; *'...indeed I am near. I answer the prayer of every caller (silent or audible) when he calls upon Me ...'* - Quran 2:186. Your whole life can change with the power of du'aa; *'du'aa is the most potent weapon of a believer, it can change fate while no action of ours ever can'* - Prophet Muhammad (pbuh). Do you want a reunion with your friend? A good job? Success in your exams? Your partner to be nice to you? Raise your hands, ask Allah for it sincerely, ask that He ultimately does what is best for you in this matter, and have complete belief that only He can give you what you want, as nothing is impossible for Him; *'when He wills anything, His only command is to say "Be!" – and it is'* - Quran 36:82. Allah guarantees to respond, one way or another. If He wills, He will give you what you want immediately, otherwise He will respond another time in another positive form or He will respond in Heaven – whatever He thinks is best for you. And above all that, Allah will love you and reward you just for asking; *'there is nothing more dear to Allah, than a servant making du'aa to Him'* - Prophet Muhammad (pbuh).

Day
164

Gaze up at the sky

Take half an hour out to lie down outside and stare up at the sky. Watch how the clouds appear to be gently moving, yet it is you with the Earth that is rotating. See the shapes the clouds form as they pass you by. Look out for birds roaming above. Know that the stars you see at night are still there during the day. Why is the sky blue? Ask yourself which direction Allah's Heaven is towards; it is somewhere out there. Escape from the plainness of the day and imagine being sat on a fluffy cloud; what would you think of our tiny planet Earth? Or would you be too busy looking elsewhere, searching for Heaven? *'Do they not look at the sky above them? How We have made it and beautified it, and there are no flaws in it?'* - Quran 50:6; *'...these are certainly signs for people who reflect'* - Quran 45:13.

Day
165

Be nice without expecting gratitude

Do something nice for three people today. Give a lift to a friend. Tell your mother you love her. Take your sibling for a hot chocolate. But the essential part is to not expect gratitude from anyone. Do these nice, selfless acts purely for Allah's love, because it pleases Him, and your purpose in life is to please Him. *'I have not created jinn and mankind (for any purpose) except to worship Me'* - Quran 51:56. Have no expectation of gratitude and returned favours from people and you will never be disappointed. Most people are ungrateful to their very Creator and Sustainer, so how can you expect them to be grateful to you? Keep giving selflessly. If you get a smile in return, that is a bonus, but unbreakable peace and happiness lies with pleasing Allah. And your reward is with Allah. *'We feed you for only Allah's pleasure. We desire no reward, nor thanks from you'* - Quran 76:9.

Day
166

Notice Allah's signs in your day

Notice Allah's signs as you go through your day. Every single thing that you experience today – the warm bed you wake up in, the sunshine seeping through your window, that nice pair of shoes you wear, the frown on the face of the bus driver as you get on, that bar of chocolate you treat yourself to, your perfect workout at the gym, the wind that blows your umbrella upside down, the darkness of the night – all of it, has been put in your day for only one reason. And that is to show you and remind you of Allah. *'Verily! In the creation of the Heavens and the Earth, and in the alternation of night and day, there are indeed signs for those who have intelligence'* - Quran 3:190; *'…"Our Lord! You did not create (all) of this without a purpose, glory be to You"…'* - Quran 3:191. To show you the greatness, kindness and power of your Creator, so that you may come to love Him and fulfil your purpose; *'I have not created jinn and mankind (for any purpose) except to worship Me'* - Quran 51:56. Take a fresh, spiritual perspective of your life, by making note of your given signs today and telling yourself how they remind you of Allah.

Day
167

Visualise Heaven in detail

Meditate for 10 minutes today and think about Heaven. Sit upright, close your eyes and monitor your breathing. Breathe in and out as slowly as possible – this will slow down your heart and relax you. Focus on what you think Heaven looks like. Be specific. Visualise: having more beauty than any woman or man on this planet; gliding through the grounds of your magnificent palace; being lost in the joyous embrace of your family and friends that had passed away, flying through the white skies of Heaven, catching shooting stars with your hands, kissing moons with your lips, swimming under waterfalls of honey and in seas of melted chocolate, being waited on by Angels who bring you fruits, wines and cakes. And, not forgetting the most spell-binding moment; imagine yourself finally meeting Allah, the Greatest. See yourself there, and smile. *'…There you shall have whatever your heart desires, and you shall have whatever you ask for. This is the hospitality from the Most Forgiving, the Most Merciful'* - Quran 41:31-32. Ask Allah for it, and you will have it, *insha'Allah* (Allah willing). *'…Indeed I am near. I answer the prayer of every caller (silent or audible) when he calls upon Me …'* - Quran 2:186. Let this be the reason for you to be happy today.

Day
168

Find ways to laugh

Find ways to laugh today. You could play a light prank on your partner, play a board game with your family, reminisce about funny incidents with your friends or watch some light-hearted videos online. Make an active effort to physically laugh whenever you can, even when you find things only mildly amusing. Laughter makes you feel good, relaxes your body, de-stresses you and improves your health. Recognise that these are small, yet meaningful, moments of happiness that Allah peppers into your life; *alhamdulillah* (all praise and thanks be to Allah). *'And if you were to count the blessings of Allah, never will you be able to count them'* - Quran 14:34.

Day
169

Your complaints are disrespecting Allah

Don't complain about anything today out of fear of disrespecting Allah. Imagine you came to know of someone who had absolutely nothing and so you gave him; a passport to a civilised country, a house, a car, some friends, food every day, an education, a job, a wardrobe full of clothes, a mobile phone, holidays and many other gifts. And that person then complains that the meal you gave today doesn't taste nice or complains about not having the latest phone. You would feel hurt and angry at the shocking ungratefulness of this person. Would you want to give him more? Each time we complain about anything, we are complaining to Allah; the One who has given us everything when we started with nothing. *'Then which of your Lord's favours will you deny?'* - Quran 55:13. The next time you are about to complain, think about how outrageous and shameless it would be, and instead say "thank you Allah". *'...And Allah will soon reward the grateful ones'* - Quran 3: 144.

Day
170

Be refined in your speech

Today, be refined in your speech. Speak no evil, do not backbite, do not be suspicious, do not argue, do not get angry, do not be unpleasant, do not hurt anyone's feelings and do not express ingratitude to Allah by complaining. Be extremely disciplined with yourself on this and you will notice your bad feelings sink low and good feelings rise to the surface. *'Blessed is the person who speaks good...'* - Prophet Muhammad (pbuh).

Day
171

Go for a short walk

Go for a short walk today. Preferably in the daylight. Walking will trigger your body's relaxation responses, clear your mind and help reduce stress. Even a short 10 minute walk will give you an immediate energy boost, improve your mood and of course, keep you fit, *insha'Allah* (Allah willing). So, put your technology away, breathe in the fresh air, and observe your surroundings – from the ground to the sky – pondering Allah's creations. *'…"Our Lord! You did not create (all) of this without a purpose, glory be to You"…'* - Quran 3:191.

Day

172

Note your positive moment of the last day

Write down one positive thing that has happened to you in the last 24 hours. It might be that you prayed all your 5 prayers and felt a sense of accomplishment and peace. Go into as much detail as you can – where you prayed and how you felt – so your brain recreates the moment and brings back those happy feelings you had. Re-read what you write throughout the day for an instant boost. Also, please Allah by thanking Him for this moment of happiness and, *insha'Allah* (Allah willing), you will have another moment tomorrow; '...*if you are grateful, I will certainly grant you more [favours]...*' - Quran 14:7.

Day
173

You're one of the most fortunate in the world

Realise, that if you are able to obtain and read this book, then you are probably in the top 20% of the most fortunate people currently in the world. You have spare money or borrowing facilities, and you've had an education to be able to read. At all times today, remember this and remember that Allah could have so easily placed you in the bottom 80%. Sincerely thank Allah. *'Then which of your Lord's favours will you deny?'* - Quran 55:13.

Day
174

Don't dwell on your worries of the future

Today, don't be engrossed in fear of the future. Don't worry about; your tasks for tomorrow, not having enough money this year, whether you will ever marry, not having children, or whether you will be free from illness in a few years. You don't know what tomorrow will bring, or even if you will be alive tomorrow. Life surprises us every day. Concentrate on the beautiful moments right now and kick out all worrying thoughts. And when, or if, tonight comes, close your eyes, say "I trust you Allah", and have complete, unshakeable trust in Him, that tomorrow He will be by your side – that is all you need. '*...And whoever places his trust in Allah, Allah is Sufficient for him, for Allah will surely accomplish His Purpose. For verily, Allah has appointed for all things a due proportion*' - Quran 65:3.

Day
175

All worries become just memories of the past

Pick a date at random from the last 10 years. Try to remember where you were on that date, what your life situation was, what your hopes were and what your happiness and sadness was. Remember the good, marvel at how you have overcome the bad, and see how far life moved on from that day. Now see how life will move on from today. Don't waste time dwelling on today's worries as you will realise again, in 10 years time, that these worries passed, making them insignificant. *'This worldly life is a trivial [fleeting] gain. Undoubtedly, the Hereafter, is really a place to live'* - Quran 40:39.

Day
176

Sleep can give more happiness than money

Make sure you get 8 hours sleep tonight – no matter what. Sleep is fundamentally linked to happiness, and a bad nights rest is sure to affect your mood. Your mind and body need enough sleep. Sleep provides the necessary energy for the day, which in turn will make you more energetic, socialise more, pray better and generally be more upbeat, which will ultimately lead to increased happiness. Studies suggest that an extra hour of sleep a day would do more for a person's happiness than a $60,000 raise in annual salary. Realise how important sleep is and that it is a great gift from Allah too, so by accepting it, your sleep becomes a form of worship. *'And remember when He made slumber fall upon you as a means of serenity from Him'* - Quran 8:11.

Day
177

Call a good friend

Call a good friend that you have not spoken to for a while. Good friendships are one of life's greatest joys and source of happiness. If you are in contact with people who spread spirituality and knowledge, exude positive vibes and generally express happiness, their goodness will rub off onto you. Follow Prophet Muhammad's (pbuh) advice and choose to call someone who is good for you; *'a person is on the religion of his companions. Therefore let every one of you carefully consider the company he keeps'*. The best friends being; *'one whose appearance reminds you of God, and whose speech increases you in knowledge, and whose actions remind you of the Hereafter'*.

Day
178

Create a To-Do list

Organise yourself and make a to-do list for today. A person who plans their day has a more productive day, and productivity increases happiness. Write down all the things you want doing today. Balance the list with worship, work and life; just like Prophet Muhammad (pbuh) used to carefully do. Allocate time for job matters, prayers, chores, spending time with family, exercising and even one of your hobbies. Now work through that list and make sure each one has a tick next to it by the end of the night. Knowing that you have had a balanced day will, *insha'Allah* (Allah willing), make you feel satisfied and content with yourself.

Day
179

Make your 5 daily prayers & you're a winner

Make your 5 daily prayers and consider yourself a winner today. As a Muslim, your sole purpose in life is to worship Allah. *'I have not created jinn and mankind (for any purpose) except to worship Me'* - Quran 51:56. One of the obligatory pillars of worship is to perform the 5 daily prayers (the others being the testimony of faith, fasting in Ramadan, performing Hajj and giving to charity). Take a few minutes out, throughout the day, to perform your 5 obligatory prayers. See these prayers as a display of your love and devotion to Allah, your Creator. You can rest tonight feeling like a winner, knowing that you have fulfilled a major part of your purpose today.

Day
180

Hydrate yourself well

Drink 2-3 litres of water today. Dehydration can cause headaches, make you feel tired and affect your mood. '...*And we created every living thing from water*' - Quran 21:30. Your body is made up of 80% water. The old water in your body needs replenishing with fresh water. This fresh water cleanses the body of toxins, revives the skin, energises the brain, and generally makes you feel rejuvenated and therefore happier. Water is essential to life and look at how Allah has made it free and amply flowing in the Earth. *Alhamdulillah* (all praise and thanks be to Allah)!

Day
181

Visualise the end of your current goals

Think of a goal you currently have, close your eyes and imagine yourself there at the end. Signing the contract for a new job? At the finishing line of a marathon? Cutting your cake on your wedding day? Receiving your graduation certificate? Speaking a new language fluently? Trekking around the world? Really go into detail. Where are you? How does the outcome look? How does it feel? What are you wearing? What are you saying? What does everyone else think? Focus on this vision for 5-10 minutes. Visualising the result of your dream will firstly, bring a moment of joy, and secondly, will motivate you to work towards your goal. Now importantly, raise your hands and ask Allah to help you with your goal; *'You alone do we worship and You alone do we seek for help'* - Quran 1:5; *'call upon Me; I will respond to you'* - Quran 40:60.

Day
182

More money will not make you happier

Get the thought that more money will make you happier, out of your head. This is something crucial to understand, as people tend to desire wealth the most in life. Having enough money for food, shelter and clothing is an important factor in happiness, and can generally be achieved by hard work. But, believe it or not, evidence states that once you have enough money to support your basic needs, your inner happiness is not significantly affected by the amount you make on top of that. Your optimism and outlook on life is what make a big difference. So spend your time today working on being positive and grateful towards your current situation, rather than wasting time on chasing more money. *'Riches does not mean, having a great amount of property, but riches is self-contentment'* - Prophet Muhammad (pbuh).

Day
183

A slower day is a peaceful day

A slower day is a peaceful day. Avoid rushing today. Relax. Cherish your moments. Drive slowly – enjoy the ride. Walk slowly – enjoy the scenery. Eat slowly – enjoy the tastes. Pray slowly – enjoy the peace. Speak slowly – enjoy your conversations. These are all graceful ways to conduct your day that will effectively reduce stress. Grace is in line with the ways of Prophet Muhammad (pbuh), and will give you opportunities to reflect on and appreciate what is around you; *'…"Our Lord! You did not create (all) of this without a purpose, glory be to You"…'* - Quran 3:191.

Day
184

Learn about the history of your country

Learn about the history of your country. What kind of houses did people live in over 200 years ago? What was the average wage? What jobs did people do? Who ruled the country? How did people shop? How did your country become multi-cultural? What was the main religion? How did war affect people? What was life like without technology? Is life much better these days? Learning something new and interesting will enrich your mind and your life. The process of gaining this knowledge will repel boredom, make you feel happier and at the same time be an act of worship as Allah commands us to seek knowledge; *'and say: `My Lord! Increase me in knowledge'* - Quran 20:114; *'travel through the Earth and observe how Allah began creation. And then Allah will produce the final creation'* - Quran 29:20.

Day
185

Ask yourself "will this please Allah?"

Before every action of yours today, ask yourself; "will this please Allah?" Let Allah be the reason for your decisions and actions. When it comes to deciding what to wear in the morning, whether to buy that bunch of flowers for your mother as you pass them in the supermarket or whether to get angry at your partner for not being home on time for dinner, ask yourself; "will this please Allah?" By putting Allah's pleasure first you are set for a successful day, as you are concentrating on the purpose of your life, always doing what is good and moral, and highly likely to disregard trivial matters that cause you unhappiness. And if you have gained Allah's pleasure, then that is better than Heaven. *'Gardens under which rivers flow, where they shall live forever, and beautiful mansions in Eternal Heaven. But the greatest bliss (happiness) is the Good Pleasure of Allah. That is the ultimate success'* - Quran 9:72.

Day
186

Write 3 things you are grateful for today

Think about 3 things you are grateful for today. Your best friends? Your ability to practice your faith? The sun shining today? Write them down on a piece of paper. Re-read and savour these 3 things throughout your day, and each time you do, show gratitude firstly to Allah, and then to those people who play a part in these blessings. Grateful people are happier people, and less prone to stress and depression. Also in Islam, half of inner happiness is to be grateful in good times, an act for which you will also be greatly rewarded by Allah. *'Therefore remember Me. I will remember you. And be grateful to Me and do not be ungrateful'* - Quran 2:152.

Day
187

Keep your inner thoughts lively

Your thoughts are like a friend who is having a conversation with you, so keep them lively and colourful today. If you sit with a friend who is constantly moaning, complaining and thinking bad about others, you wouldn't like it and would want to get away. Think of your thoughts like that; a friend talking to you. When you have an argument with your husband, don't go on and on about it within and instead tell yourself a joke about it. When you're feeling tired, tell yourself you've had enough sleep and to liven up. When it starts raining, laugh and tell yourself to get wet. Stop the moaning and negativity, and turn the conversation to something uplifting, entertaining and inspiring. *'Blessed is the person who speaks good...'* - Prophet Muhammad (pbuh).

Day
188

Nothing in life lasts

Remind yourself today that nothing lasts. This is the sweetness and bitterness of this life. Every sadness you have will not last. Every joy that you have will not last. Don't get attached to these everyday moments – the laughter of your son, the loneliness of your nights, the warmth of your partner, the suppleness of your cheeks, the pain from your cancer, the stable bricks of your home. Life ends, along with everything in it. Know today that every moment has wings, so be sure to savour your joyful moments before they fly away, and ignore your sad moments knowing that they too will fly away. *'This worldly life is a trivial [fleeting] gain. Undoubtedly, the Hereafter, is really a place to live'* - Quran 40:39.

Day
189

Live simply

Live today in a simple manner, like Prophet Muhammad's (pbuh) example. Don't eat too much, don't buy expensive branded food, stay away from designer clothes and only get what you need. Try not to want what you don't need. Live simply. Because firstly, it is the Islamic way and Allah is testing you on how you use your wealth; are you selfish or selfless? *'The son of Adam will not pass away from Allah until he is asked about five things…'*, the fourth being; *'how did he spend his wealth…'* - Prophet Muhammad (pbuh). And secondly, living simply has proven to make people happier as: you will stress less about maintaining your standard of living, the fewer your possessions the less your burdens and, the more you spend your excess on the poor instead the better you will feel. *'Whatever good you spend, He will replace it [with better]….'* - Quran 34:39.

Day
190

Spend time with family or friends

Finish your work and chores early today to go and spend time with your family or a group of friends. According to research (Journal of socio-economics), relationships are worth more than $100,000 a year because increasing social involvements increases life satisfaction more than what an extra $100,000 a year would. Investing your love in family and friends is of course, if done for Allah's pleasure, also a form of worship to Him. *'Allah will ask on the Day of Judgment: "Where are those who loved each other for the sake of My glory? Today – on a day when there is no shade but mine – I shall shade them with My shade"'* - Prophet Muhammad (pbuh).

Day
191

Ask Allah for whatever you wish for

When you wish for something, big or small, ask Allah. It's as simple as that. Allah says; *'call upon Me; I will respond to you'* - Quran 40:60. Your whole life can change with the power of du'aa; *'du'aa is the most potent weapon of a believer, it can change fate while no action of ours ever can'* - Prophet Muhammad (pbuh). Worried about an interview today? Ask Allah to make it easy. Hoping dinner is enjoyable today? Ask Allah. Want a good night's sleep? Ask Allah. Wishing you don't feel so tired right now? Ask Allah. Raise your hands, ask Allah for it sincerely, ask that He ultimately does what is best for you in this matter, and have complete belief that only He can give you what you want, as nothing is impossible for Him; *'when He wills anything, His only command is to say "Be!" – and it is'*- Quran 36:82. Allah guarantees to respond one way or another. If He wills, He will give you what you want immediately, otherwise He will respond another time in another positive form or He will respond in Heaven – whatever He thinks is best for you. And above all that, Allah will love you and reward you just for asking; *'there is nothing more dear to Allah, than a servant making du'aa to Him'* - Prophet Muhammad (pbuh).

Day
192

Spend time in a natural environment

Spend at least 30 minutes outside today. Try and go to a beautiful, natural environment such as the beach, a park, the river or in the woods. Light deprivation will make you feel tired. But stepping outside into the daylight releases brain chemicals, serotonin and dopamine, which will clear your mind, boost your energy and improve your mood. This moment will also give you an opportunity to reflect and ponder over Allah's existence and how He has placed His wonderful signs wherever you look; *'to Allah belong the east and the west, wherever you turn, there is the face of Allah…'* - Quran 2: 115.

Day
193

Learn about dreams

Learn about dreams today. You dream every single night, so ask yourself, what causes us to have good dreams and bad dreams? Why do we dream? Do they mean anything? Research into how science explains dreams and what Islam says about them. Learning something new and interesting is important for happiness. Novelty broadens your mind, keeps you away from boredom and creates self-satisfaction within. See your learning process as a form of worship to Allah too, as He commands us to seek knowledge and reflect. *'And say: My Lord increase me in knowledge'* - Quran 20:114; *'...these are certainly signs for people who reflect'* - Quran 45:13.

Day
194

Believe that you'll have your desires in Heaven

Write down 5 things that you dream to have, and truly believe that you will have them in Heaven. Do you desire; eternal peace? A wonderful family? The ability to ski on water? An adventurous life? An endless supply of doughnuts? '... *In Heaven, there will be whatever the heart desires, whatever pleases the eye* ...' - Quran 43:71. Ask Allah for them; '...*indeed I am near. I answer the prayer of every caller (silent or audible) when he calls upon Me* ...' - Quran 2:186, and one day you will have them, *insha'Allah* (Allah willing). Let this be the reason for you to smile today.

Day
195

Help someone solely for Allah's pleasure

Think of someone you can help today, solely for the love of Allah. Can you help babysit for your sister-in-law? Wash the dishes for your mother? Take an old person shopping? Massage your father's feet? There will surely be something you can do. If Allah is pleased, then you have achieved your purpose of life today (of worshipping Allah), and in turn, you will be pleased. *'Allah will ask on the Day of Judgment: "Where are those who loved each other for the sake of My glory? Today – on a day when there is no shade but mine – I shall shade them with My shade"'* - Prophet Muhammad (pbuh).

Day
196

Plan something fun for this month

Plan something fun for this month. A holiday with the family? A weekend break with your partner? A climb up a mountain on your own? A picnic by the lake? An evening at the bowling alley? A dinner party for family? Put a date into your diary. The positive anticipation of a forthcoming event is scientifically proven to make you feel better. So whenever you need a boost of happiness, remind yourself of what is to come, *insha'Allah* (Allah willing). *'And if you were to count the blessings of Allah, never will you be able to count them'* - Quran 14:34.

Day
197

Note a recent positive moment

Write down one positive thing that has happened to you in the last 24 hours. It might be, the good time you had when you took your niece to the park? Go into as much detail as you can – what you played and how you laughed – so your brain recreates the moment and brings back those happy feelings you had. Re-read what you write throughout the day for an instant boost. Also, please Allah by thanking Him for this moment of happiness and, *insha'Allah* (Allah willing), you will have another moment tomorrow; *'...If you are grateful, I will certainly grant you more [favours]...'* - Quran 14:7.

Day
198

Every moment is an enchanting moment

Recognise that there is gold in every moment. There is magic taking place when you sleep, as you travel into an unimaginable life in your dreams. The moment you open your eyes, the world is waiting to see how you will make it a better place. Whilst you talk to and smile at your close one, the love from your heart pours out and warms the air. When you cry alone in your room, Heaven sets its place for you, eager to see your smiles. As you pray, your soul rises with joy, people await to see whether you will say a prayer for them, and Allah turns Himself to hear you. Every moment is an enchanting moment, and you don't need background music to feel it or a cinema screen to see it. Cherish these moments. *'And if you were to count the blessings of Allah, never will you be able to count them'* - Quran 14:34.

Day
199

The Greatest is always with you

If you are in a state of sadness today, remind yourself; *'Be not sad. Surely Allah is with us'* - Quran 9:40. Close your eyes, hold your heart and truly feel His presence: *'... remember Me. I will remember you...'* - Quran 2:152. Allah, the Greatest, is with you. Always. And *'...Allah is sufficient for us...'* - Quran 3:173. Find comfort in these words.

Day
200

Write a gratitude letter to someone

Write a gratitude letter to your partner, parent, sibling or friend. In words, put down all the things that you are thankful for, which you rarely speak of. It could be the fact that your husband provides for you, the way he listens to your problems, how he brings you a glass of water at night? It may be the lovely meals your mother always has ready on the table when you come home, how she never says no to your requests, is always full of good advice? When writing this you will recognise how lucky you are to have this person in your life. The recipient of the letter will feel great at being appreciated. And also, Allah will be pleased and you will be rewarded by Him. *'He who does not thank people, does not thank Allah'* - Prophet Muhammad (pbuh).

Day
201

Make extra time for exercise

Give yourself an extra hour this morning to exercise. Go for a run round the block, go to the gym, run up and down the stairs at home or do a body workout in your bedroom. Do it with a smile, even if you don't feel like it. Scientific research states that exercise is one of the most important factors in making us feel happy. Certain chemicals in your body, like endorphins, increase drastically after a workout, which results in giving you a happy feeling. And generally, people who exercise are healthier, look trimmer, think more clearly and sleep better. Prophet Muhammad (pbuh) also advised us to look after our bodies, which are a gift from Allah, by implementing exercise into our lives. *'Then which of your Lord's favours will you deny?'* - Quran 55:13.

Day
202

Pick a room & have a clear out

Pick a room and have a clear out. Get rid of clutter, things you haven't used in a year, or don't need. Bags, letters, clothes, shoes, ornaments, spare utensils in the kitchen, excess jewellery, unused furniture, extra towels – give them away to charity or throw them away. Be ruthless. You will not miss this extra baggage. Don't feel that you might need it one day, live for today and trust in Allah for tomorrow. Removing your attachment to material possessions will take away the physical disorder in your life to make room for calmness, freedom and clarity of thinking; help the people you donate to; and lead you to living a simple, non-extravagant life as Islam promotes. *'The son of Adam will not pass away from Allah until he is asked about five things…'*, the fourth being; *'how did he spend his wealth…'* - Prophet Muhammad (pbuh). Our excess wealth is there only to test us – use it for doing good, and from now on, try to only buy what you need. *'…The righteous is the one who…gives wealth, in spite of love for it, to relatives, orphans, the needy…'* - Quran 2:177.

Day
203

Closely observe life in front of you

Today, pay close attention to the things around you and reflect. On your way to work, listen to the noise of the traffic, watch those walking by to their destination, notice the fluttering of the leaves in the trees. Watch how a smile forms on the face of the lady who serves you coffee or your friend's body language as she talks. *'To Allah belong the east and the west, wherever you turn, there is the face of Allah...'* - Quran 2:115. Escape from thoughts of yourself and let your mind marvel at the true magnificence Allah has placed in front of you.

Day
204

Your heart is a ticking timer

Listen to and feel your heart beat. It almost sounds like a ticking timer. Well, it is. Each beat of your heart is another second passed. The alarm has been set and when it rings, that is when your death will arrive. Know that the seconds of your life are slipping away. With each heartbeat you are getting closer to that meeting with Allah. Today, don't waste time. Start now in satisfying your purpose in life (*'I have not created jinn and mankind (for any purpose) except to worship Me'* – Quran 51:56). Thank Allah for all He has blessed you with, praise Him for His beauties, love Him, worship Him, trust Him, be nice to others for Him, live a pleasant day for Him, avoid sin for Him, remember Him, and look forward to the moment you will meet Him and His Heaven. And if you find yourself dwelling on negative things, then hold your hand to that timer again to remind yourself. *'The one who remembers death most often and the one who is well-prepared to meet it; these are the wise; honourable in this life and dignified in the Hereafter'* – Prophet Muhammad (pbuh).

Day
205

Diarise your tasks

Diarise all your things to do. If you need to attend an upcoming meeting, send an email, renew your car insurance, call a friend, make holiday plans, or whatever it is, assign dates and times for you to deal with these tasks. It is better to use an electronic calendar so you can easily rearrange your tasks. When each day comes, discipline yourself to deal with the tasks on that day, seeking ease from Allah on the matters; *'You alone do we seek for help'* - Quran 1:5. This simple method of scheduling will help you be organised and prevent you from feeling stressed, and therefore happier, *insha'Allah* (Allah willing).

Day
206

Accept the life Allah has given you

Accept everything in your life that Allah has decided for you. Your achievements, your failures, your past woes, your recent happiness. Know that *'what hit you, could not have missed you and what missed you could not have hit you'*, as said by Prophet Muhammad (pbuh). Destiny is destiny, fate is fate. Know that nothing has happened, or nothing will happen, except what Allah meant it to be. No human being or thing can change your blessings or hardships. Only lawful du'aa can make changes to what is already written; *'du'aa is the most potent weapon of a believer, it can change fate while no action of ours ever can'* - Prophet Muhammad (pbuh). Therefore, profusely make du'aa that Allah does what is best for you, and then without fear or regrets, rest your heart with Allah, be patient in bad times, be grateful in good times, and accept His decree as the most-wise decision for you – Allah is the Most-wise, He makes the best decisions and His decision-making ability cannot be beaten, so trust Him. Acceptance of Allah's decisions, by being grateful or patient, is a key factor to inner contentment and true faith. 'Say: *"nothing shall ever happen to us except what Allah has ordained for us. He is our Mawla (protector)."* And in Allah let the believers put their trust' - Quran 9:51. You are exactly where Allah wants you to be, so accept your life; be patient, be grateful.

Day
207

Give some money to the needy

Spend a little money today on the poor and needy. Even if you can only afford a dollar, still give, as it is the good intention to please Allah and His creation that counts; *'verily actions are by intention'* - Prophet Muhammad (pbuh). With even a dollar, you will be making a positive difference to lives in the world, cleansing and soothing your soul, pleasing Allah, and making room for more blessings to come into your life. *'Do not withhold your wealth, (for if you do), Allah will withhold His blessings from you'* - Prophet Muhammad (pbuh); *'whatever good you spend, He will replace it [with better]....'* - Quran 34:39.

Day
208

Renew your life's purpose

Take two minutes, in the morning, afternoon and evening, to stop, close your eyes, and renew your life's purpose. *'I have not created jinn and mankind (for any purpose) except to worship Me'* - Quran 51:56. You were not created to make lots of money, to decorate your home, to go on holidays, to win arguments or to be selfish with pleasure. You were created to solely worship Allah, by doing things that please Him. Say "I am here to worship Allah" and focus on gaining His love throughout your day, by simply doing good things in His name and for His pleasure. Speak nice words, smile at others, make your prayers, help a local charity, be kind, say the truth, spread knowledge, thank Allah, and refrain from sin. If you have His love, then you will have eternal happiness, *insha'Allah* (Allah willing).

Day
209

You have more blessings than hardships

Be happy with what you have right now, no matter how bad your situation is. Even if you are currently going through a tough jobless period, a tragic death in the family or a heart-breaking divorce, believe it or not, there will be a lot more blessings in your life than hardships which can make you happy – your warm home, your caring family, your lovable children, your perfectly working body, your deep faith, your hopeful education, your fear-free residence in society. *'Certainly, with every hardship there is ease'* - Quran 94:5. The control of your happiness is in your mind. Train your mind today to focus and zoom in on the good things in your life. Block out or minimise all thoughts of your hardships. And certainly don't waste time waiting for your troubles to disappear or wishes to be fulfilled before you feel you can be happy. Prophet Muhammad (pbuh) spoke about this issue very eloquently; *'...If the son of Adam has one valley, he will wish that he had a second, and if he had two valleys, he would wish that he had a third. The stomach of the son of Adam will be filled only with dust (i.e., he is never satisfied)...'.*

Day
210

Focus on making lives around you happier

Today, don't dwell on your own happiness. Take the pressure off yourself and focus on making the lives around you happier. Make coffees for your colleagues, say nice words to your friends, offer to run an errand for your mother, spend some quality time with your siblings, help your neighbour with the gardening, give some bread to the local ducks. Making others happy will, by default, make you feel happy too and it will also please Allah; both of which will give comfort to your soul. '*...And do good (to others); surely Allah loves the doers of good*' - Quran 2:195.

Day
211

Imagine how life could be worse

Today, if you are unhappy about something, really think about how it could be worse and thank Allah. If your children are giving you grief, imagine being of those who can never have children and will never experience the sheer joy having kids has brought you. *Alhamdulillah* (all praise and thanks be to Allah). If your complaint about your husband is that he is unromantic, imagine if he was abusive and a drunken alcoholic like many men out there. *Alhamdulillah*. If you are unhappy with the size of your house, really picture yourself living under a tin roof in India. *Alhamdulillah*. Prophet Muhammad (pbuh) famously said; *'look at those people who have less than you and never look at those who have more grants than you, this will ensure that you will not depreciate Allah's favours'*. Breathe a sigh of relief and smile at your fortune.

Day
212

Take steps towards your life ambitions

What would your ideal life on Earth be like – your dream existence? Write it down on a piece of paper clearly. Would you live in a bungalow? Work as a teacher? Be married? Have 3 children? Spend your weekends hill hiking? Cook for your family in the evenings? Travel around the world? Spend your days following the way of life of Prophet Muhammad (pbuh)? Dreams and ambitions reignite sparks, and instil new enthusiasm and pleasure into life. After penning your ideal life on this paper, stick it to your fridge, and vow to take steps, each day, to make your dream-on-Earth come true. Say *'bismillah'* (in the name of Allah), ask Allah for help, and start today. *'You alone do we worship and You alone do we seek for help'* - Quran 1:5.

Day
213

Sprinkle 10 pleasures into your day

Think of 10 simple pleasures you can give yourself every day. Jot them down. It could be; eating chocolate, drinking a cup of tea, watching the sunset, reading a book, getting into your warm bed, playing with your child, taking a stroll around your block, hugging your partner, sending a nice message to a loved one, watching a funny video online, having a hot shower, lighting a candle whilst you pray. Once written down, make effort to sprinkle those 10 pleasures into your day today. That's a lot of joy in the day that probably does not get the appreciation it deserves. *Alhamdulillah* (all praise and thanks be to Allah). *'And if you were to count the blessings of Allah, never will you be able to count them'* - Quran 14:34.

Day
214

Every person you meet has a story of sadness

Look at every person you cross today, pause, and know that upon every cheek you see run tears. Everyone is being tested. You cannot see the hidden depths of people's sorrows; past, present, or future, including those of your friends and family, but consider that their story, despite how they may appear, is more painful than yours – broken hearts, loneliness, abuse, addiction, confusion, depression, loss, money troubles. Step away from your own sadness, unify with others and lend them a brave smile, a kind word or a silent prayer. They may need it – today or one day. *'Do you think that you will enter Paradise without such [trials] as came to those who passed away before you? They were afflicted with severe poverty, ailments and were shaken, until the Prophet [pbuh] and those with him who had faith said "when will the help of Allah come?" Surely, the help of Allah is near'* - Quran 2:214.

Day

215

Write about your past like it's yet to happen

Transport your mind to 5 years ago from today, and write a short paragraph to yourself about what is about to happen in the next 5 years. Focus on the happy moments but also mention the sad. Are you going to get married? Have a baby? Will you lose somebody? Will you start a new career? Are you going to move to a different town? Will you fail your exams? Are you going to meet a new best friend? Will you go on a journey of a lifetime? Read this to yourself as though you are reading it 5 years earlier and are yet to experience the things you mention. Now, come back to the present, and notice how Allah had placed moments in your life of both joy and sorrow for your benefit. So that you may learn to remain faithful to Him by being patient in bad times and grateful in good times; both of which would earn you a place in Heaven. See how the next 5 years from today may hold many good times for you to look forward to and be grateful for – be excited. And perhaps some bad times will come too that you will survive through and be patient with – take comfort. Say *bismillah* (in the name of Allah) and begin the next 5 years of your life today. Promise to keep your love for Allah true by being patient in bad times and being grateful in good times, and your next 5 years will be a success. '*…If you are grateful, I will certainly grant you more [favours]…*' - Quran 14:7; '*I have rewarded them this day for their patience and faithfulness: they are indeed the ones that have achieved bliss…*' - Quran 23:111.

Day
216

Turn off all technology for an hour

Switch off all technology this evening for at least one hour. Phone, laptop, computer and the TV. Turn away from the millions of distractions these devices can bring, as well as proven depression, stress and sleep disorders. Spend quality time with your family over dinner. Spend some time on a hobby. Go out for a walk. Read a book. Have a hot, candle-lit bath. Anything, but don't be tempted to switch your electronics back on. Really enjoy your time away from technology and instead soak in the simple and wonderful gifts Allah has given you. *Alhamdulillah* (all praise and thanks be to Allah). '*And if you were to count the blessings of Allah, never will you be able to count them*' - Quran 14:34.

Day
217

Utter glorifications of Allah

Utter glorifications of Allah today. Say *Allahu akbar*, (Allah is the Greatest), 100 times. Because He is the Greatest as He created the world, Heaven and you. Say *SubhanaAllah*, (Glory be to Allah) 100 times. Because glory rightfully be to Him for all the beauty and miracles that surround you. Say *Alhamdulillah*, (All praise and thanks be to Allah) 100 times. Because of the countless blessings He has given you. Your soul will find peace in satisfying its purpose of loving and remembering Allah. *'Surely, in the remembrance of Allah do hearts find rest'* - Quran 13:28.

Day
218

Spend quality time with someone you love

Take an hour out today to spend quality time with someone who you love – friend or family. Bake a cake with your friend? Go for a night stroll with your wife? Listen to your child read? Have tea and cake with your grandfather? Go shopping with your mother? Allah has created us in such a way that we have a natural human need to be close and intimate with other human beings. Having strong and loving relationships fulfil that need, which in turn pours tranquillity into your life. *'And Allah has made for you from your homes a place of rest'* - Quran 16:80.

Day
219

See the world via a travel programme

Watch a travel programme today. These will be readily available online. Perhaps a documentary on a backpacker's journey through Brazil. Or a man's journey to India through the slums of Bombay. Or maybe about a traveller's visit to remote villages in Africa. Or an explorers trek through the Amazon rainforest. *'Say [o Muhammad]: "travel on the Earth..."'* - Quran 6:11. It might be that you cannot afford to travel far and wide, but you can still be transported across the globe visually, and benefit from seeing the natural wonders Allah has created and seeing how other people in other countries live and love. There is a great world out there, spread the wings of your mind, escape from your sadness and fly into another land for a fresh perspective on life. *'..."Our Lord! You did not create (all) of this without a purpose, glory be to You"...'* - Quran 3:191.

Day
220

Write 3 things you are grateful for today

Think about 3 things you are grateful for today. Your sense of humour? Your university education? Your decent car? Write them down on a piece of paper. Re-read and savour these 3 things throughout your day, and each time you do, show gratitude firstly to Allah, and then to those people who play a part in these blessings. Grateful people are happier people, and less prone to stress and depression. Also in Islam, half of inner happiness is to be grateful in good times, an act for which you will also be greatly rewarded by Allah. *'Therefore remember Me. I will remember you. And be grateful to Me and do not be ungrateful'* - Quran 2:152.

Day
221

Believe your wishes will come true in Heaven

Write down 5 things that you dream to have, and truly believe that you will have them in Heaven. Do you desire; eternal joy? A large family? A unicorn? The ability to swim oceans? A fleet of supercars? Happiness for everybody? '... *In Heaven, there will be whatever the heart desires, whatever pleases the eye ...*' - Quran 43:71. Ask Allah for them, '...*indeed I am near. I answer the prayer of every caller (silent or audible) when he calls upon Me ...*' - Quran 2:186, and one day you will have them, *insha'Allah* (Allah willing). Let this be the reason for you to smile today.

Day
222

Go for a stroll somewhere pleasant

Go for a 30 minute stroll somewhere pleasant – along the river, in the park, by the beach. This will refresh your mind and body. And when you look at the objects of nature – the trees, birds, the sun, mountains, flowers – remind yourself that these things are in constant worship of Allah. As you witness these things in worship, be inspired and worship Allah too. Your heart will find peace, *insha'Allah* (Allah willing). *'Do you not see that all within the Heavens and on Earth prostrate to Allah — the sun, the moon, the stars; the hills, the trees, the animals; and a great number of mankind?'* - Quran 22:18.

Day
223

Ask Allah for whatever you want

If you want something, ask. Ask Allah for it. Today. It is as simple as that. Allah reassures you; *'…indeed I am near. I answer the prayer of every caller (silent or audible) when he calls upon Me …'*- Quran 2:186. Your whole life can change with the power of du'aa; *'du'aa is the most potent weapon of a believer, it can change fate while no action of ours ever can'* - Prophet Muhammad (pbuh). Hoping for a successful day? Ask Allah. Want to find a bargain in the sales? Ask Allah. Hoping your bank approves a loan? Ask Allah. Want happiness in your marriage? Ask Allah. Raise your hands, ask Allah for it sincerely, ask that He ultimately does what is best for you in this matter, and have complete belief that only He can give you what you want, as nothing is impossible for Him; *'when He wills anything, His only command is to say "Be!" – and it is'*- Quran 36:82. Allah guarantees to respond, one way or another. If He wills, He will give you what you want immediately, otherwise He will respond another time in another positive form or He will respond in Heaven – whatever He thinks is best for you. And above all that, Allah will love you and reward you just for asking; *'there is nothing more dear to Allah, than a servant making du'aa to Him'* - Prophet Muhammad (pbuh).

Day

224

Stop & stare

Today, stop and stare – at everything and every moment around you. *'Verily! In the creation of the Heavens and the Earth, and in the alternation of night and day, there are indeed signs for those who have intelligence'* - Quran 3:190; *'...'Our Lord! You did not create (all) of this without a purpose, glory be to You'...'* - Quran 3:191. Take your time to enjoy each of the countless rich moments in your day – like the ones William Henry Davies speaks about in his famous poem 'Leisure':

WHAT is this life if, full of care,
We have no time to stand and stare?
No time to stand beneath the boughs,
And stare as long as sheep and cows:
No time to see, when woods we pass,
Where squirrels hide their nuts in grass:
No time to see, in broad daylight,
Streams full of stars, like skies at night:
No time to turn at Beauty's glance,
And watch her feet, how they can dance:
No time to wait till her mouth can
Enrich that smile her eyes began?
A poor life this if, full of care,
We have no time to stand and stare.

Day
225

Meditate for 15 minutes

Sit down in a quiet corner for 15 minutes and meditate. Close your eyes. Breathe in deeply. Breathe out slowly. Breathe in and imagine that Allah is placing your soul into your body. Hold your breath and know that it is only Allah that sustains your breathing and, ultimately, your life. Breathe out and imagine that your soul is being released to fly back to its Creator. Find comfort in the knowledge that your soul will one day return to its true home. To Allah. *'Surely, to Allah we belong, and to Him we shall return'* - Quran 2:156. Concentrate for these 15 minutes and do not let your mind wander, and if it does, gently bring it back to your breathing and your thoughts of Allah. This is a perfect way to step away from the chaos of life, bring perspective and calmness to your mind and reconnect your soul with your Creator. *'Surely, in the remembrance of Allah do hearts find rest'* - Quran 13:28.

Day
226

Visit your family

Save that extra work or errand for another day and go visit family. One of the things that can produce the greatest happiness is when enjoying time with loved ones. And when you are with your loved ones, put your technology and other distractions away, and really savour this special bonding moment – be attentive, listen, smile, laugh, play, converse. Also remember, that the time you spend with your family is pleasing to Allah and therefore a form of worship; *'the best of you is the one who is best to his family'* - Prophet Muhammad (pbuh).

Day
227

Wake up early

Get up early today. Prophet Muhammad (pbuh) said; *'the early morning has been blessed for my ummah'*. The earlier you wake up, the more blessed your day will be, the less rushing around you will be doing and the more time you will have to fit in important things like prayers, work, exercise, hobbies, family time and quiet contemplation. Of course, sleep is essential, so also sleep early tonight. The recommended time to sleep is after the Isha prayers, and the best time to rise is for the Tahajjud and Fajar (pre-dawn) prayers. Allah says; *'and [We] have made the night as a covering [through its darkness], and have made the day for livelihood'* - Quran 78:10-11.

Day
228

Be patient through your sadness

Be patient with the sadness that you carry today and know that your patience and trust in Allah alone may lead you to a place in Paradise. *'I have rewarded them this day for their patience and faithfulness: they are indeed the ones that have achieved bliss...'* - Quran 23:111. View the level of patience you show in Allah – by accepting and having firm trust in His decisions, and then continuing to please Him – as the test you need to take and pass in order to achieve eternal happiness. Trust Allah, pray, be nice to others regardless, smile, give your riches, be thankful, enjoy His bounties, refrain from sin. Envisage the end goal. *'And the Hereafter is better for you than the [first] life'* - Quran 93:4. When you think about the shortness of life, patience does seem to be a very small price to pay in exchange for Heaven.

Day
229

Plan a different activity for this weekend

Plan to go to a local event this weekend. There will be something going on in your area; a funfair, a farmers market, a charity event or a festival. If there is not, arrange an outdoor get together with friends or family – a long countryside walk, a visit to the beach, or a play around in the local park. Plan it today, and look forward to the refreshing change in activity and scenery – this will boost your spirits. *'Then which of your Lord's favours will you deny?'* - Quran 55:13.

Day
230

Turn today into a day of worship to Allah

When doing anything today, remind yourself of your purpose in life. *'I have not created jinn and mankind (for any purpose) except to worship Me'* - Quran 51:56. You have been put on Earth only to worship Allah. Everything you do in your day should be for the love of Allah. So today, turn your day into a day of worship to Allah, by continuing your normal lawful tasks, but doing them solely to please Him. Minute by minute. Go to work and make an honest living; Allah loves the righteous and commands us to work to sustain our lives of servitude. Eat a healthy breakfast, lunch and dinner; so that you have enough energy to do acts that please your Lord. Make all your 5 prayers; Allah loves the submissive. Be nice and loving to all you meet; Allah loves the kind. Go see natural beauty and praise Allah; Allah loves the one who glorifies Him. Thank Allah when you have drank; Allah loves the grateful. Resist sin; Allah loves the good. Beg Allah to forgive you when you make mistakes; Allah loves the one who repents. Raise your hands and ask Allah for whatever you wish for right now; Allah loves the one who asks. Throw out all your sadness, worries and fears, by being patient and trusting Allah completely to eternally take care of you and all you love; Allah loves the one who is patient and trusts Him. Remember Allah at all times; Allah loves those that remember Him. And sleep well tonight; so you are recharged to worship Him again tomorrow. Focussing on your life's purpose will take your mind off unrelated problems, increase your love for Allah and Allah's love for you, and open up the doors of Heaven. This is peace.

Day
231

Look good, smell good, feel good

Make sure you are well-groomed and well-dressed for the day, even if you are staying in the house. Wear your favourite clothes, your best perfume and even some pretty jewellery. Look good, smell good, feel good – it is as simple as that. It is also within Islamic etiquette to be clean, neat and well-dressed. In response to a man's comment about the man wearing nice clothes and shoes, Prophet Muhammad (pbuh) responded; *'Allah is Beautiful and likes beauty'*. The most important time of your life is right now, as the past has gone and the future may just never come. This moment is special; dress like it is so you feel like it is.

Day
232

Spend some money for the pleasure of Allah

Spend some money today for the pleasure of Allah. Perhaps you could buy a sandwich for a homeless man, give a few coins to the local mosque, make an online donation to a charity, or buy a rose for your mother. '...*The righteous is the one who...gives wealth, in spite of love for it, to relatives, orphans, the needy...*' - Quran 2:177. Be it a tiny amount or a lot, know that whatever it is, you are making someone smile, bringing comfort to your heart, worshipping Allah, and by default, Allah will multiply what you give tremendously with reward. '*The likeness of those who spend for Allah's sake is like a grain which grows seven ears, every single ear has a hundred grains. Allah multiplies (increases the reward of) for whom He wills...*' - Quran 2:261.

Day

233

Eat or drink at a scenic place

Have breakfast, lunch or a late afternoon dessert of cake and coffee outdoors somewhere. Drive to the beach, or any other natural setting, like a lake, river or mountain. Light deprivation will make you feel tired. But stepping outside into the daylight releases brain chemicals, serotonin and dopamine, which will refresh your mind, boost your energy and improve your mood. If it is too cold to be sitting outside, stay in your car but still enjoy the scenery. Enjoy the peaceful moment to reflect on the Earth that Allah has gifted you with. *'Or who has made the Earth firm to live in; made rivers in its midst; set mountains on it, and has placed a barrier between the two seas? [Can there be another] god besides Allah?...'* - Quran 27:61.

Day
234

Remember Allah with every breath

There is an opportunity to think of Allah with every breath; use it. Allah mentions, at various points in the Quran, that He has left signs of His existence, His power and His mercy, in everything. *'To Allah belong the east and the west, wherever you turn, there is the face of Allah…'* - Quran 2:115. Pick out and explore these signs as much as you can today. The magical sunrise, the tweeting birds, the love from your husband, the warm food on your plate, your deep thoughts, your amazing ability to talk, a strangers mysterious smile, your complex phone, the remarkable growth of your child, the loyal beat of your heart, the intricate workings of society. Think, and say *subhanAllah* (glory be to Allah) and *alhamdulillah*, (all praise and thanks be to Allah). Remembrance of Him is your reason to breathe and your path to peace. *'Surely, in the remembrance of Allah do hearts find rest'* - Quran 13:28.

Day
235

Note a positive moment of the last 24 hours

Write down one positive thing that has happened to you in the last 24 hours. It might be that sunset walk you took yesterday evening? Go into as much detail as you can – what the weather was like and how the sky appeared – so your brain recreates the moment and brings back those happy feelings you had. Re-read what you write throughout the day for an instant boost. Also, please Allah by thanking Him for this moment of happiness and, *insha'Allah* (Allah willing), you will have another moment tomorrow; *'...if you are grateful, I will certainly grant you more [favours]...'* - Quran 14:7.

Day
236

Exhibit gentleness in your character

Exhibit gentleness in your character today. Speak softly using only pleasant words. Smile regularly. Be well-mannered. Behave gracefully. And do noble deeds. And if someone upsets you, still respond with gentleness. Be like this because Allah loves the gentle, people love the gentle, and you will love the gentle in you. By nature, peace will follow and enter your heart, *insha'Allah* (Allah willing). '*...Allah is gentle and He loves gentleness. He rewards for gentleness what is not granted for harshness and He does not reward anything else like it'* – Prophet Muhammad (pbuh); '*those who repress anger, and who pardon men; verily Allah loves the good-doers'* - Quran 3:134.

Day
237

Fit some exercise into your day

Get some exercise in today. Even if it is just for 30 minutes. Go for a brisk walk around the block, a bike ride, or run up and down the stairs at home. Scientific research states that exercise is one of the most important factors in making us feel happy. Certain chemicals, like endorphins, increase drastically after a workout, which results in giving you a happy feeling. And generally, people who exercise are healthier, look trimmer, think more clearly and sleep better. Prophet Muhammad (pbuh) also advised us to look after our bodies, which are a gift from Allah, by implementing exercise into our lives. *'Then which of your Lord's favours will you deny?'* - Quran 55:13.

Day
238

Be inspired by the Prophet's patience

Whenever you feel that life is tough, remember one important thing – the trials of Prophet Muhammad (pbuh). He was the most beloved of Allah, yet was beaten, driven out of Mecca, lost his son and most of his daughters, often tied a stone around his stomach to lessen the pangs of hunger, was accused of being a madman, and faced many more terrible afflictions. Yet still his patience, his trust in Allah to be doing what is best and his continuing love for Him was unshakable. Be inspired by the greatest man to have walked the Earth. Realise that if Allah's beloved was tested, then of course you will be tested too, but know that Heaven is earned with patience and trust in Allah's will. *'I have rewarded them this day for their patience and faithfulness: they are indeed the ones that have achieved bliss...'* - Quran 23:111.

Day
239

Post an inspirational quote to your neighbour

Write and post an inspirational quote into your neighbour's letterbox. It could be a verse from the Quran; *'certainly, with every hardship there is ease'* - 94:5; *'be not sad. Surely Allah is with us'* - 9:40. Or it could be a saying from someone famous; *'change your thoughts and you change your world'* - Norman V Peale. Or perhaps some wise words your mother once taught you. This is your random act of kindness. A few words that may brighten your neighbour's day, make you feel good about it and grant you reward from Allah. *'Blessed is the person who speaks good…'* - Prophet Muhammad (pbuh).

Day
240

Write 3 things you are grateful for today

Think about 3 things you are grateful for today. Bumping into an old friend this afternoon? Being able to concentrate on your prayers today? Having the opportunity to do a good deed and help someone out? Write them down on a piece of paper. Re-read and savour these 3 things throughout your day, and each time you do, show gratitude firstly to Allah, and then to those people who play a part in these blessings. Grateful people are happier people, and less prone to stress and depression. Also in Islam, half of inner happiness is to be grateful in good times, an act for which you will also be greatly rewarded by Allah. *'Therefore remember Me. I will remember you. And be grateful to Me and do not be ungrateful'* - Quran 2:152.

Day
241

Say yes when you'd normally say no

Say yes to something today that you would usually say no to. By saying no to offers, invites and opportunities, you are closing doors on wonderful experiences and new possibilities of finding joy. Have you always said no to learning how to drive because of nerves? Say yes today and book your first lesson – driving will open up new channels of freedom and endless experiences. Do you usually say no to going out for a walk because it's too cold? Say yes today, wrap up well and go out – being in the cold outdoors will clear your mind and leave you feeling refreshed. Have you recently made an excuse not to have coffee with an old friend because you can't be bothered? Say yes today and arrange a date with him or her – you may receive some useful advice on a personal matter and share some good jokes. Instead of the usual no, actively say yes more often, go with the flow and you will likely be left feeling pleasantly surprised. Also, these are opportunities of happiness and remembrance of Allah that have been placed into your life, so do remember to thank Him for them. *'Then which of your Lord's favours will you deny?'* - Quran 55:13.

Day
242

Plan a treat for yourself

Plan to treat yourself today and look forward to it. You could plan to; make your favourite dinner, buy yourself some perfume, go for a pleasant stroll, watch your favourite program on TV, spend some alone time, have a hot bath or dive into a good book. Today is about indulging in yourself. Smile. And be grateful for such accessible pleasures. *Alhamdulillah* (all praise and thanks be to Allah). *'…If you are grateful, I will certainly grant you more [favours]…'* - Quran 14:7.

Day
243

Learn about the science behind the internet

Find out how the internet works, if you don't already know. It is astonishing how we use it every day and could not imagine life without it, yet most of us don't know how it works. How does an email you send end up with a recipient in another country? How does the internet allow you to buy things? How is information stored? Who was the brains behind this? Learning something new and interesting will enrich your mind and your life. The process of gaining this knowledge will repel boredom, make you feel happier and at the same time be an act of worship, as Allah commands us to seek knowledge; *'and say: `My Lord! Increase me in knowledge'* - Quran 20:114.

Day
244

Talk to Allah at Tahajjud time

Pray Tahajjud, the pre-Fajar prayers, tonight. Prophet Muhammad (pbuh) said: *'our Lord descends to the lowest Heaven during the last third of the night, inquiring: "Who will call on Me so that I may respond to him? Who is asking something of Me so I may give it to him? Who is asking for My forgiveness so I may forgive him?"'* Rise in the middle of the night, half an hour before the morning prayer (Fajar salah), and make 2 or 4 nafil prayers. Have an open chat with Allah about your life, your wants, your regrets, your worries and your hopes. Pour out your heart, without restraint. He is listening, ready to respond. Praying Tahajjud is not an easy task. It is a rare accomplishment and the feeling of peace that follows throughout the day is unrivalled.

Day
245

Reject all negative thoughts

Do not allow any negative, bad or depressing thoughts to enter your head or words to exit your mouth today. No anger, no jealousy, no sulking, no sadness, no envy, no arguing, no ungratefulness, no impatience and no complaining. Be disciplined. Be firm with yourself. If you sense one of these feelings creeping into your mind, throw it out immediately and try to replace it with a positive thought, or at least a neutral thought. If you see your friend driving a flashy sports car, rather than feeling or expressing jealousy, be happy for her fortune and admire her car. If you find yourself stuck in a traffic jam, rather than being impatient, take the time to savour this quiet moment to yourself. If your partner is in a bad mood tonight, rather than being annoyed, remind yourself of all the good moods he or she has been in, in the past. By nature, peace will follow and enter your heart, *insha'Allah* (Allah willing). *'Blessed is the person who speaks good...'* - Prophet Muhammad (pbuh).

Day
246

Remove excess belongings in your home

Today begin efforts to live simply. Take a scan of one of your rooms in the house and get rid of anything that you feel you don't need. Giveaway or throwaway books you would not read again, extra make-up, excess clothes, useless ornaments, empty boxes, needless furniture, spare utensils, excess jewellery, extra towels. Think of the Prophet (pbuh) and his companions, and how they gave much of their belongings away and lived contentedly with meagre possessions. Be free from the shackles of material possessions. As you get rid of weight in your home, you will feel that you are getting rid of weight in your heart and mind – making room for peace, clarity of thinking and calmness. *'Whoever has extra provision should give from it to the one who has no provision...'* - Prophet Muhammad (pbuh).

Day
247

Start learning something new

Think of one thing you have always wanted to learn and be determined to take an hour out today to start. Have you always wanted to learn a new language? Learn some words online. Have you always wanted to learn how to sew? Go out and get a starter-sewing kit. Have you always wanted to learn how to drive? Sit in a friend's car and play around with the controls. New challenges open doors for new pleasures in your life. And above that, see this as a form of worship to Allah, because Allah commands us to seek knowledge; *'and say: "My Lord! Increase me in knowledge'* - Quran 20:114.

Day
248

Plan an event for charity

Pick a charity and make a plan today to help raise money for them. It can be very easy. Perhaps you could organise a walk around the largest local park and get all participants to raise money via sponsorships? Or maybe you could get your friends to help you bake cakes to then sell on for cash? Or suppose you could organise a fundraising dinner for just family and friends? Make it fun, and try to get as many people involved, both young and old. Spending your time making small differences to those in need will bring a natural comfort to your heart, purify your soul, make others happy, take your mind away from your own problems and of course, help fulfil your purpose of worshipping Allah. '...*And do good (to others); surely Allah loves the doers of good*' - Quran 2:195.

Day
249

Be content with your lot in life

Today, be content with your lot in life – *ridha bi al-qadha*, as Islam calls it. It is a major requirement of happiness to be content with all that you have; the size of your bank account, your 2 bedroom house, your small family, your average looks or your basic salary. Know that; *'what hit you, could not have missed you and what missed you could not have hit you'*, as said by Prophet Muhammad (pbuh). Destiny is destiny, fate is fate. Know that nothing has happened, or nothing will happen, except what Allah meant to be. No human being or thing can change your blessings or hardships. Only lawful du'aa can make changes to what is already written; *'du'aa is the most potent weapon of a believer, it can change fate while no action of ours ever can'* - Prophet Muhammad (pbuh). Therefore, profusely make du'aa that Allah does what is best for you in matters of your lot, and then accept what He has given you, be patient with the little, be grateful for the big, and accept His decree as the most-wise and best decision for you. Allah is the Most-wise, He makes the best decisions and His decision-making ability cannot be beaten, so trust Him. Contentment with Allah's decisions, by being grateful or patient, is a key factor to inner happiness and true faith. You are in the exact position that Allah wants you to be in, so accept your lot; be patient, be grateful. To help with this, make the prayer that Prophet Muhammad (pbuh) used to make; *'O Allah, make me content with what you have provided me, send blessings for me therein, and place for me every absent thing with something better'*.

Day
250

Get some ice cream with loved ones

Go get some ice cream with your friends, family or kids today. It doesn't need to be time-consuming or pre-planned. Pick up whoever is interested and walk, if you can, to your nearest ice cream parlour. Enjoy a new flavour and a chat with your companions. A random and simple way to boost your mood. *Alhamdulillah* (all praise and thanks be to Allah). *'And if you were to count the blessings of Allah, never will you be able to count them'* - Quran 14:34.

Day
251

Your hardships are a blessing

If you are feeling down today, wondering why God, the most Merciful, is putting you through hardships, then realise that this hardship is actually a blessing. Allah tells us that we will all be tested; *'most definitely We will test you with some fear and hunger, some loss in goods, lives and the fruits (of your toil)…'*- Quran 2:155. Even His most beloved, Prophet Muhammad (pbuh), was tested with hardships, more than you ever will be. But sometimes Allah puts you through the sad times because He knows that it is when you are at your lowest that you are most likely to; find Him, turn to Him for comfort, realise your purpose in life, recognise that Allah is the Giver and Taker, and then submit and be patient with whatever He has willed for you, and perhaps afterwards, be grateful to Him when He makes life better. All this will then ultimately result in you earning a place in Heaven, *insha'Allah* (Allah willing). *'…But give good news to those who patiently persevere. Those who, when any difficulty befalls them, say: 'Surely, to Allah we belong and to Him we shall return. Those are the ones upon whom are blessings and mercy from their Lord and it is those who are rightly guided'* - Quran 2:155-157. The sadness you experience in this life, is actually for your happiness in the afterlife. *'…He will give you [something] better than what was taken from you…'* - Quran 8:70. And remember; *'Allah does not burden a soul more than it can bear'* - Quran 2:286.

Day
252

Explore a new natural surrounding

Find a new beach, park, river, or countryside that you have not been to and plan to go explore it either today, or within this week. Follow Allah's command to travel; *'say [O Muhammad]: "travel on the Earth..."'* - Quran 6:11. Exploring a new part of Allah's creation will give you a fresh source of enjoyment and renew your appreciation of Allah and the natural beauty He has blessed you with. *'..."Our Lord! You did not create (all) of this without a purpose, glory be to You"...'* - Quran 3:191.

Day
253

Write 'B' on your hand, for *Bismillah*

Grab a marker, and write a 'B' at the back of your hand. 'B' for *bismillah* (in the name of Allah). Each time you see the B, you will be reminded to say *bismillah* before every task you begin; waking up, starting your car, taking a bite of your sandwich, beginning work, sending an email, getting out of your chair, starting to cook, hugging your child. This regular utterance will bring divine blessing into your activities, but most importantly, it will remind you amidst your daily worries, that your purpose in life is to worship Allah, and therefore everything you do should be in His name, for Him. *'I have not created jinn and mankind (for any purpose) except to worship Me'* - Quran 51:56.

Day
254

Share 3 good things that happen today

At the end of the day, share with a friend, three good things that happen today. Keep an eye out for them. It may be that hilarious joke your brother tells you, that delicious slice of pie you eat or the praise you receive from your boss. Spot the good things that happen in the day – however small – smile, and thank Allah. *'So take what I have given you and be of the grateful ones'* - Quran 7:144.

Day
255

Lift people's moods by being positive

Show positivity to everyone you cross today, to lift their moods. Be the one that brings a smile to people's faces because you are cheerful, full of good words and radiate a fresh energy. Don't be the one who brings other's moods down because you are depressing, complain all the time and are never smiling. Even if you feel low, stay positive for your family or for the cashier that serves you at the supermarket and see that as your charitable deed for the day. By nature, this will make you feel good too. *'Do not dismiss certain acts of kindness by deeming them to be insignificant, even if such an act is to meet your brother with a smiling face, for that is a deed which might weigh heavily in your scale of good deeds'* - Prophet Muhammad (pbuh).

Day
256

Make decisions quickly

There will be decisions to make today, make them quickly. Granted, some decisions do require deep thought, but don't waste time on non-life changing decisions like; what to wear? What to eat? What to do later? Nothing drastic will happen if you choose to wear a blue top instead of a red one. Your life will not change if you decide on a salad for lunch today rather than a sandwich. Both staying in and going out tonight have their benefits – pick any. Making snap decisions will free the space in your head, and a clear mind leads to a happy mind. So briefly ask Allah to make you choose what is best, trust Him, go with your gut instincts and don't look back. Allah makes the final decision on what will happen in your day anyway, and accepting this is key to contentment and faith. *'Say: "Nothing shall ever happen to us except what Allah has ordained for us. He is our Mawla (protector)" And in Allah let the believers put their trust'* - Quran 9:51.

Day
257

Note a positive moment of the last 24 hours

Write down one positive thing that has happened to you in the last 24 hours. It might be that fantastic meal you had? Go into as much detail as you can – the flavours you experienced and how you felt eating it – so your brain recreates the moment and brings back those happy feelings you had. Re-read what you write throughout the day for an instant boost. Also, please Allah by thanking Him for this moment of happiness and, *insha'Allah* (Allah willing), you will have another moment tomorrow; *'...if you are grateful, I will certainly grant you more [favours]...'* - Quran 14:7.

Day
258

Accept all that Allah has decided for you

Accept what Allah has decreed for you. Allah is the Most-wise and He makes the best decisions – His decision-making ability cannot be beaten – so ask Him to do what is best for you and trust Him. And know that whatever situation you are in right now, and whatever are Allah's reasons behind it, it is ultimately for the best. Whether you have just given birth to a beautiful girl or have just lost your daughter, it is for the best, as you have the perfect opportunity to exhibit either patience in Allah (by maintaining firm trust in your Lord's decision and continuing to please Him) or gratitude to Allah (by thanking Him and continuing to please Him); both of which will open up the doors of Heaven as a reward, *insha'Allah* (Allah willing). *'...And it may be that you dislike a thing which is good for you and that you like a thing which is bad for you. Allah knows but you do not know'* - Quran 2:216; *'...if he (the believer) is granted ease of living, he is thankful; and this is best for him. And if he is afflicted with a hardship, he perseveres; and this is best for him'* - Prophet Muhammad (pbuh). Acceptance of Allah's decree, by being grateful or patient, is a key factor to inner contentment and true faith. You are exactly where Allah wants you to be, so accept your life; be patient, be grateful.

Day
259

Gaze at the night sky

Tonight, grab a blanket, go outside, lay down somewhere and gaze at the stars, the moon and, if you can, the planets – Mercury, Mars, Venus, Jupiter and Saturn; all of which can be seen with the naked eye. Count the stars, try to work out how far away they must be, what the atmosphere in space must be like and how great Allah is to have created billions of stars, and many planets and moons, just in our galaxy alone – galaxies of which there are billions too. Or perhaps just stare out and lose yourself in this vast number of twinkling beads in the sky, looking down at you. What a simple, beautiful and magical moment that will take your breath away. Truly, how great is Allah and how small is our Earth. '...*"Our Lord! You did not create (all) of this without a purpose, glory be to You"*...' - Quran 3:191; '...*these are certainly signs for people who reflect*' - Quran 45:13

Day
260

Write 3 things you are grateful for today

Think about 3 things you are grateful for today. Your intelligence? The roof on your head? The fact that no harm has come your way lately? Write them down on a piece of paper. Re-read and savour these 3 things throughout your day, and each time you do, show gratitude firstly to Allah, and then to those people who play a part in these blessings. Grateful people are happier people, and less prone to stress and depression. Also in Islam, half of inner happiness is to be grateful in good times, an act for which you will also be greatly rewarded by Allah. '...If you are grateful, I will certainly grant you more [favours]...' - Quran 14:7.

Day
261

Try fasting

Try fasting today. Fasting is one of the best ways to detox your soul and body. Your soul is nourished as you teach it self-discipline and restraint from not just food, but also sinful acts, and focussing on remembering your Creator. *'Fasting is not (just abstaining) from eating and drinking, but also from vain speech and foul language. If one of you is being cursed or annoyed, he should say: "I am fasting, I am fasting"'* - Prophet Muhammad (pbuh). And as for your body, scientists have found that fasting gives the body a well-needed break, and time to rejuvenate and cleanse itself. Allah loves those who fast, so intend to cleanse your soul and body, primarily for the pleasure of Allah, and when breaking your fast, be happy knowing that many benefits have come from this.

Day
262

Think of Allah the most

Today, change what you usually think about the most, to Allah. *'Laa illaha illallah'* means *'there is no diety worthy of worship except Allah'*. What do you think of the most, and therefore; what is your heart most attached to, what makes you most happy and most sad, what would break you if it disappeared? If, throughout the day, you find yourself thinking about your husband, your job, your children or your upcoming holiday more than you are thinking of your Lord, then, practically, you are making these things your *illah* (the object of your worship). That must change immediately to be a true believer, as our bodies and our hearts belong to Allah and we were only created to worship Him; *'I have not created jinn and mankind (for any purpose) except to worship Me'* - Quran 51:56. Not only that; Allah is the Greatest and Eternal, therefore make Him your *illah* and He will never disappoint you – unlike people and materials. So continue to love your husband, continue to concentrate on work, continue to look after your children and continue to make holiday plans with your family but do it because it pleases Allah. Make the pleasure of Allah your daily focus and motivation. Practically, what is your *illah*? Say Allah, prove that today and surely you will find peace. *'...But those that truly believe, love Allah more than anything else...'* - Quran 2:165.

Day
263

Be inspired by other's success stories

Think of your current goal in life and seek inspiration from other people's success stories. Do you want to be a top journalist? Read a current journalist's success story online. Do you want to be a good mother? Watch an online video on the secrets of successful mothers. Do you want to be a successful entrepreneur? See how the best entrepreneurs went from rags to riches. Or do you simply aspire to be a better Muslim? In that case, read about how individuals found Islam, or better still, read the Prophet's (pbuh) biography. Whichever it is, be inspired by others, inject some fresh motivation into your life and ask Allah to help you reach your goal – He can and He will, *insha'Allah* (Allah willing). *'You alone do we worship and You alone do we seek for help'* - Quran 1:5; *'call upon Me; I will respond to you'* - Quran 40:60.

Day
264

Meditate

Meditate for 10 minutes; in the morning, afternoon and evening. Spend those 10 minutes, sat in a quiet corner, with your eyes closed, concentrating on your breathing. Strictly focus on each breath and with each one say "Allah", reminding yourself that the reason that Allah keeps you alive and breathing is so that you may worship Him. If you find your mind drifting away, gently bring it back to focus on your breathing and Allah again. This is a perfect way to step away from the chaos of life, bring perspective and calmness to your mind and reconnect your soul with your Creator. *'Surely, in the remembrance of Allah do hearts find rest'* - Quran 13:28.

Day
265

Ask Allah for whatever you want today

If you want something today, the first thing you can do as a believer, is raise your hands before Allah and ask Him; the Giver of everything. Allah reassures you; *'...indeed I am near. I answer the prayer of every caller (silent or audible) when he calls upon Me ...'* - Quran 2:186. Your whole life can change with the power of du'aa; *'du'aa is the most potent weapon of a believer, it can change fate while no action of ours ever can'* - Prophet Muhammad (pbuh). Do you want to have a stress-free day at work? Want to be able to concentrate on your revision? Have an enjoyable time at your relative's party tonight? However big or small, whenever you want it, pause, raise your hands, ask Allah for it sincerely, ask that He ultimately does what is best for you in this matter, and have complete belief that only He can give you what you want, as nothing is impossible for Him; *'when He wills anything, His only command is to say "Be!" – and it is'* - Quran 36:82. Allah guarantees to respond, one way or another. If He wills, He will give you what you want immediately, otherwise He will respond another time in another positive form or He will respond in Heaven – whatever He thinks is best for you. And above all that, Allah will love you and reward you just for asking; *'there is nothing more dear to Allah, than a servant making du'aa to Him'* - Prophet Muhammad (pbuh).

Day
266

Photograph 3 things that make you happy

Take a photo of 3 things that make you happy. It could be your partner, your daughter's smile, your home, your bed, your city, your prayer mat, your breakfasts, your car, your scenic walks, the mug you have a cup of tea in, your book collection. These are hidden treasures that generally go unnoticed day to day; treasures that should be savoured at every given moment. Collate the photos and keep them as your screen savers or put them beside your desk. Each time you see them remind yourself of the happiness they bring, savour the thought and smile. *Alhamdulillah* (all praise and thanks be to Allah). *'And if you were to count the blessings of Allah, never will you be able to count them'* - Quran 14:34.

Day
267

Notice Allah's signs in your day

Notice Allah's signs as you go through your day. Every single thing that you experience today – your face as you look in the mirror, the headache you develop in the afternoon, the cat you see running into the bushes, the hot cup of tea that warms your body, the accident you witness on your way home from work, the innocent smiles on your children's faces, the tiredness in your body after a long day, the hot bath you manage to take at night – all of it, has been put in your day for only one reason. And that is to show you and remind you of Allah. *'Verily! In the creation of the Heavens and the Earth, and in the alternation of night and day, there are indeed signs for those who have intelligence'* - Quran 3:190; *'..."Our Lord! You did not create (all) of this without a purpose, glory be to You"...'* - Quran 3:191. To show you the greatness, kindness and power of your Creator, so that you may come to love Him and fulfil your purpose. *'I have not created jinn and mankind (for any purpose) except to worship Me'* - Quran 51:56. Take a fresh, spiritual perspective of your life, by making note of your given signs today and telling yourself how they remind you of Allah.

Day
268

Nothing in this life is forever

If you are feeling sad today, be comforted by the certainty that nothing in this life is forever. Your laughter will end but then, so will your tears. Be patient; ask Allah to do good by you, say "I trust you Allah to be doing what is best for me", then continue with your devotion to Him, and He will surely reward you with Heaven. *'I have rewarded them this day for their patience and faithfulness: they are indeed the ones that have achieved bliss...'* - Quran 23:111; *'Oh mankind, indeed you are ever toiling towards your Lord, painfully toiling... But you shall meet Him'* - Quran 84:6.

Day
269

Believe you'll have your desires in Heaven

Write down 5 things that you dream to have, and truly believe that you will have them in Heaven. Do you desire; eternal happiness? The return of a long-lost loved one? A pony? The ability to fly? Magnificent beauty? Unconditional love? A direct conversation with Allah? '... *In Heaven, there will be whatever the heart desires, whatever pleases the eye ...*' - Quran 43:71. Ask Allah for them; '*indeed I am near. I answer the prayer of every caller (silent or audible) when he calls upon Me ...*' - Quran 2:186, and one day you will have them, *insha'Allah* (Allah willing). Let this be the reason for you to smile today.

Day
270

Get some exercise in today

Get some exercise in today. Even if it is just for 30 minutes. Go for a brisk walk round the block, a run in the park, or run up and down the stairs at home. Scientific research states that exercise is one of the most important factors in making us feel happy. Certain chemicals, like endorphins, increase drastically after a workout, which results in giving you a happy feeling. And generally, people who exercise are healthier, look trimmer, think more clearly and sleep better. Prophet Muhammad (pbuh) also advised us to look after our bodies, which are a gift from Allah, by implementing exercise into our lives. *'Then which of your Lord's favours will you deny?'* - Quran 55:13.

Day
271

Eat moderately

When eating your meals today, don't fill your stomach to the rim. Prophet Muhammad (pbuh) emphasised a habit of eating less, to prevent sickness, disease and feelings of laziness. *'Nothing is worse than a person who fills his stomach. It should be enough for the son of Adam to have a few bites to satisfy his hunger. If he wishes more, it should be: one-third for his food, one-third for his liquids, and one-third for his breath'*. Try this today, and, *insha'Allah* (Allah willing) you will feel more energetic, upbeat and healthy.

Day
272

You are a perfect creation

You are a perfect creation – think about this all day. Don't look at anyone else, just yourself. Think about how your eyes allow you to see all the beauty of life and nature that is around you. How your teeth are made tough for you to chew delicious meals. How your fingers and thumbs allow you to pick up your phone and connect with your friends across the globe. How your legs bend at the knees and hips, allowing you to walk to wherever you want and sit whenever you feel tired. How your soul allows you to feel that unexplainable emotion called love. How your mind enables you to think and then put those thoughts into action. How you are respected and dignified compared to insects and animals. You are blessed. A walking, talking, smiling miracle. Greater than anything man has ever invented. *'We have indeed created humankind in the best of molds'* - Quran 95:4. Your body and soul is a gift to you from Allah. Really appreciate it at every moment today and thank Allah. *Alhamdulillah* (all praise and thanks be to Allah).

Day
273

Turn your hardships into blessings

Turn your hardships into blessings. Think of all the things that you are unhappy about. Now bite your tongue and do not complain. Raise your hands and ask Allah to do what is best for you in these matters; *'call upon Me; I will respond to you'* - Quran 40:60. Say: "I trust you Allah to be doing what is best for me". And then without fear, rest your heart with Allah, be patient in bad times, be grateful in good times, accept His decree as the most-wise and best decision for you, and continue to love and please Him. Allah rewards the one who is suffering but remains patient, with Paradise. There, your hardships have become blessings. *'Peace be upon you, because you persevered in patience! Excellent indeed is the final home (Paradise)!'* - Quran 13:24.

Day
274

Invite someone for dinner

Invite someone round to share your meal tonight and show some hospitality. See this as your act of charity today. There are many benefits you will see from such a simple act; your heart will find enjoyment in having company and seeing a smile on the face of your guest, this selflessness will focus your attention away from your worries and, above all of that, you are pleasing Allah because showing hospitality to a guest is a command from Allah and was common behaviour of the Prophet (pbuh). *'…And do good (to others); surely Allah loves the doers of good'* - Quran 2:195.

Day
275

Promise to think, speak, do, positive things

First thing in the morning, go to the mirror and talk to yourself. Look yourself in the eye and say; "today, I promise to think, speak and do only positive things. And I promise to block any negative thoughts, words and actions". Now sincerely keep that promise, if not for your own happiness, then at least for the pleasure and love of your Lord. *'...And do good (to others); surely Allah loves the doers of good'* - Quran 2:195; *'and speak good to people'* - 2:83; *'so take what I have given you and be of the grateful ones'* - 7:144; *'and in Allah let the believers put their trust'* - 9:51.

Day
276

Expect & act what you want to feel

Today, expect and act what you want to feel. This is crucial. At first, it may seem that expectations make no difference to how you feel and that you do act the way you feel. But the surprising truth is, that we tend to feel whatever we expect and we tend to feel the way we act. Feelings follow after expectations and actions. If you expect happiness in the day and act happy then you will feel happy, as your positive expectations and intentions will automatically make you look out for even the tiniest good moments and filter out the bad ones, and your upbeat actions will lift your mood. If you expect sadness in the day and act sad then you will feel sad as your negative expectations will automatically make you look out for even the tiniest bad moments and filter out the good ones, and your downbeat actions will drag your mood down. Do you want to feel happy with the day? Then firstly ask Allah for it – 'Call upon Me; I will respond to you' Quran 40:60 – believe that you will feel happy, expect happy, and act happy; smile as you drive, laugh at jokes, bring a spring to your steps, sit upright, cherish moments. Do you want to feel loving? Then firstly ask Allah for it, believe you will feel loving, expect to be loving, and act loving; show kindness, be affectionate and put warmth and in your voice. Do you want to feel physically energetic? Then firstly ask Allah for it, believe you will feel energetic, expect energy, and act energetic; speed up your walk, put liveliness into your voice and straighten up. By changing your expectations and actions into positive ones, the feelings inside you will soon follow the lead, insha'Allah (Allah willing).

Day
277

Look up at the sky often

At every opportunity today, escape from the trivialities of life, go outside and simply look up at the sky. Watch the clouds float across and imagine being taken away with them to see the wonders of the rest of the world. Ponder as to what is above and beyond the sky and know that the promised Heaven is somewhere out there. *'In a lofty Paradise, where they shall neither hear harmful speech nor falsehood. Therein will be a running spring. Therein will be thrones raised high, and cups set at hand. And cushions set in rows, and rich carpets (all) spread out'* - Quran 88:10-16. Let this moment of escapism fill you with joy.

Day
278

Note your positive moment of the last day

Write down one positive thing that has happened to you in the last 24 hours. It might be the praise you received from your boss at work? Go into as much detail as you can – what he said and how you felt – so your brain recreates the moment and brings back those happy feelings you had. Re-read what you write throughout the day for an instant boost. Also, please Allah by thanking Him for this moment of happiness and, *insha'Allah* (Allah willing), you will have another moment tomorrow; *'…if you are grateful, I will certainly grant you more [favours]…'* - Quran 14:7.

Day
279

Drink plenty of water

Drink 2-3 litres of water today. It is proven that dehydration can make you feel fatigued, grumpy, cause headaches and impact on your ability to think. Your body is made up of 80% water. The old water in your body needs replenishing with fresh water. This fresh water cleanses the body of toxins, revives the skin, energises the brain, and generally makes you feel rejuvenated, and therefore happier. Water is essential to life. And look at how Allah has made it free and amply flowing in the Earth. *Alhamdulillah* (all praise and thanks be to Allah)! *'...And We created every living thing from water'* - Quran 21:30.

Day
280

Write a gratitude letter to Allah

Write a gratitude letter to Allah. Put down as many of your blessings you have received in the past year that you can think of. A fully functioning body. Intelligence to speak, read, and write. A good job. Residency in a civilised society. Good reliable friends. Having the latest phone. Your loving parents. A nice home. The steady rhythm of your heart. Your driver's license. Your perfect vision. The fun days out in the sun. Your remembrance of Allah. Being able to keep all the fasts last Ramadan. Some great meals. The beautiful sunsets you were able to witness. Let's face it, you will never be able to write every single blessing down. *'And if you were to count the blessings of Allah, never will you be able to count them'* - Quran 14:34. See how you have much to be smiling about? And you have pleased Allah by thanking Him; *'so take what I have given you and be of the grateful ones'* - Quran 7:144.

Day
281

Clear out a room

Pick a room and have a clear out. Get rid of clutter and the things you have not used in a year or don't need. Bags, letters, clothes, shoes, ornaments, spare utensils in the kitchen, excess jewellery, unused furniture, extra towels. Give it away to charity or throw it away. Be ruthless. You will not miss this extra baggage. Don't feel that you might need it one day; live for today and trust in Allah for tomorrow. Getting rid of your attachment to material possessions will take away the physical disorder in your life to make room for calmness, freedom and clarity of thinking; help the people you donate to; and lead you to living a simple, non-extravagant life as Islam advises. *'Whoever has extra provision should give from it to the one who has no provision'* - Prophet Muhammad (pbuh).

Day
282

Smile all day

Smile all day, even if it is forced. Remarkably, by physically smiling, you instantly release positive signals and thoughts to yourself and it becomes very difficult to breed negative thoughts. If your face is smiling then eventually your heart will smile too. At the same time, smiling at others will boost their happiness too and, more importantly, will also please Allah. *'Do not think little of any good deed, even if it is just greeting your brother with a cheerful smile'* and; *'to smile in the face of your brother is charity given on your behalf'* - Prophet Muhammad (pbuh).

Day
283

Keep your state of mind content

Today, focus on creating a calm and content mind, despite what chaos may be happening on the outside. Cold weather, your income, the size of your house, the way you look, the bad traits of your partner, your hyperactive children, the rudeness of the waitress at dinner tonight – life on the outside cannot always be controlled, but your state of mind, the most important factor to your happiness, can be controlled. You are the master of your happiness. Realise this. So shift your focus away from the impossible of trying to make external life perfect and instead focus on being content within, by having positive thoughts, refusing to breed worry or stress, and maintaining perspective on your life's purpose. *'I have not created jinn and mankind (for any purpose) except to worship Me'* - Quran 51:56.

Day
284

Life is a journey from Allah to Allah

As you carry out your daily tasks today, remember that life is ultimately a journey from Allah to Allah. Nothing else. *'Surely, to Allah we belong, and to Him we shall return'* - Quran 2:156. Spend your day as though you are actually on your way back to Allah; please Allah, fill your bank of good deeds, detach your heart from materials and people, and keep the journey to your Lord at the forefront of your mind so that you don't get sucked in by the insignificant worries or distractions of the day. Look forward to the day you will return to the Greatest.

Day
285

Help someone

Think of someone you can help today. Make a monetary donation to a charity? Give some old clothes to a charity shop? Cook for your family? Take your child out somewhere fun? Go grocery shopping with your elderly neighbour? There will be an endless list of good things you can do today. It has been scientifically proven that helping others plays a big part in your own happiness. There is natural human feeling of peace and comfort that enters you when you see another person smile and be at ease because of you. And if you help for the sake of Allah, then you will feel tenfold better as you are fulfilling your life's purpose by pleasing Him. *'...And do good (to others); surely Allah loves the doers of good'* - Quran 2:195.

Day
286

Plan a trip to a museum or castle

Start planning a trip to a museum or castle for some time this month. Such places of history easily transport your imagination back to the years and centuries before you. Even if you cannot go, imagine what it was like living in the past eras? Really stretch your imagination to any time and any country, and for a moment pretend that you are there in the past – fighting as a French soldier in the world war against the Nazis, working in a British coal mine for 12 hours a day, making a fire with stones and sticks as you prepare a meal for your ten children in India, being a maid to Cleopatra in Egypt, or even walking alongside Prophet Muhammad (pbuh) in Arabia as his companion. Think about this throughout the day. Broadening your mind to a life outside of your own will bring you a new form of pleasure, make you grateful for modern ease, and also help you reflect on the varieties of existence that Allah has created. *'Travel through the Earth and observe how Allah began creation. And then Allah will produce the final creation'* - Quran 29:20.

Day
287

Sleep well tonight

Sleep enough tonight. Ideally 8 hours. Sleep plays a vital role on your daily moods. Your mind and body need enough sleep. Sleep provides the necessary energy for the day, which in turn will make you more energetic, friendlier, pray better and generally be more upbeat, which will ultimately lead to increased happiness. Studies suggest that an extra hour of sleep a day would do more for a person's happiness than a $60,000 raise in annual salary. Allah has gifted us with night, in order to rest. Accept that blessing with open arms and by doing so you are also turning sleep into a form of worship to Allah. *'It is Allah who has made the night for you to rest...'* - Quran 40:61.

Day
288

Go out to a natural surrounding

Go out into the countryside, the coast or some other natural scenery today. Don't be constricted by the narrowness of your buildings. Light deprivation will make you feel tired. But stepping outside into the daylight releases brain chemicals, serotonin and dopamine, which will refresh your mind, boost your energy and improve your mood. Allah recommends that you go out and travel; *'say [O Muhammad]: "travel on the Earth..."'* - Quran 6:11. So go. Go walk along that beach and free your soul like the bird that swims and sings in the sky. Go walk through the countryside pondering over Allah's creation; glorifying Him. *'And they think deeply about the creation of the Heavens and the Earth, [saying] "Our Lord! You did not create (all) of this without a purpose, glory be to You"...'* - Quran 3:191.

Day
289

Slowdown & enjoy moments

Resolve today to not rush with anything and take time to enjoy moments. Drive slowly and enjoy the ride – ignoring the desire to beat traffic lights. Eat slowly and really enjoy the explosive tastes in your mouth. Talk slowly when conversing and take pleasure from interacting with another being. If you have too much to do in the day, ruthlessly get rid of the tasks that are not worth your unhappiness this day. A fast-paced life is a recipe for stress and depression. Slow down, take pleasure in the present moments and reflect on all that surrounds you. *'Verily! In the creation of the Heavens and the Earth, and in the alternation of night and day, there are indeed signs for those who have intelligence'* - Quran 3:190.

Day
290

Organise a collection for the local refuge

Contact 10 of your family and friends today and ask them to donate unused toys, clothes and toiletries for you to give to the local women's refuge or such. This selfless kindness will naturally make the recipient happy, make you happy, make the ones that donated happy, and most importantly, will please Allah – which therefore helps fulfil your life's purpose. *'Whoever does good equal to the weight of an atom (or a small ant), shall see it'* - Quran 99:7.

Day
291

Thank people with 'jazakAllahu khayrun'

When someone does something nice for you today, thank them by saying; '*jazakAllahu khayrun*' (may Allah reward you with good). Be it if someone gives you a sweet, helps you unload your trolley, compliments you, or passes you the salt from across the table. Prophet Muhammad (pbuh) said; '*whoever has a favour done for him and says to the one who did it, "jazakAllahu khayrun" has done enough to thank him*'. By thanking people for the little things you are also thanking Allah for the little things, for which He will be pleased, and then so will you. '*He who does not thank people, does not thank Allah*' - Prophet Muhammad (pbuh).

Day
292

Be thankful for the modern era you live in

Be thankful for the modern era you live in. If you are able to have hot showers, eat a variety of ethnic foods, use a computer, watch world news, make phone calls, drive from A to B, read varied books, microwave food instantly, and travel abroad with ease, then you are living better than a king or queen had done 400 years ago, in the times when hygiene was poor, entertainment was limited, and technology was non-existent. Look around you today, pay close attention to each luxury you have which was not around in the past, and say *alhamdulillah* (all praise and thanks be to Allah) for the progression and ease you currently find yourself in. *'Then which of your Lord's favours will you deny?'* - Quran 55:13.

Day
293

Everything is a loaned gift from Allah

Today, realise that everything you have in your life, is not yours, but is a loaned gift from Allah. Your healthy body, your parents, your lovely siblings, your flash car, your great job, your hearing, your favourite dress, that bag of sweets in your drawer; all of it is a loaned gift from Allah and is not yours to keep forever. They are temporary gifts and each gift will, one day, certainly be taken back by Allah – your brother might die before you, you might lose your leg in an accident, your hearing might deteriorate with age, you might get fired from work, your favourite dress might ruin in the wash or you might just pass away yourself before any of these events can happen. This is the reality. So spend today cherishing and enjoying everything Allah has gifted you with. Be thankful for the gifts. And mentally be prepared to one day, sooner or later, say goodbye to each gift with the contentment and satisfaction that you took only the best from them. *'Surely, to Allah we belong, and to Him we shall return'* - Quran 2:156.

Day
294

Imagine being in Heaven

Think of the final destination; Heaven. Close your eyes and imagine yourself there. Be specific. Visualise: having more beauty than any woman or man on this planet; gliding through the grounds of your magnificent palace; being lost in the joyous embrace of your family and friends that had passed away, flying through the white skies of Paradise, catching shooting stars with your hands, kissing moons with your lips, swimming under waterfalls of honey and in seas of melted chocolate, being waited on by Angels who will bring you fruits, wines and cakes. And, not forgetting the most spell-binding moment; imagine yourself finally meeting Allah, the Greatest. Go as wild as you want with your imagination but even then Prophet Muhammad (pbuh) said that; *'Allah says: "I have prepared for My righteous slaves that which no eye has seen, no ear has heard and it has never crossed the mind of man"'*. Ask Allah to make your daydreams come true; *'…indeed I am near. I answer the prayer of every caller (silent or audible) when he calls upon Me …'* - Quran 2:186, and one day they will come true, *insha'Allah* (Allah willing). Let this be the reason for you to smile today.

Day
295

Note 3 things you are grateful for today

Think about 3 things you are grateful for today. Simply being alive? Having someone to give love to and receive love from? Being able to get to bed early tonight? Write them down on a piece of paper. Re-read and savour these 3 things throughout your day, and each time you do, show gratitude firstly to Allah, and then to those people who play a part in these blessings. Grateful people are happier people, and less prone to stress and depression. Also in Islam, half of inner happiness is to be grateful in good times, an act for which you will also be greatly rewarded by Allah. *'Therefore remember Me. I will remember you. And be grateful to Me and do not be ungrateful'* - Quran 2:152.

Day
296

Be happy with the decisions of Allah

If there is something you are not happy about, be happy about it purely because Allah wanted things to be this way. You may be feeling unhappy about the fact that you are single, or that you are not in an ideal job, or that you are ill. But this is what Allah has decreed for you, and He is the Most-wise and makes the best decisions. Raise your hands, ask Him to do whatever is best for you in this matter and He will certainly do what is best for you; *'call upon Me; I will respond to you'* - Quran 40:60. And as an expression of your love for Him, be content with His will, be patient, be grateful for everything else and say "I trust you Allah". *'But it may happen that you hate a thing that is good for you, and it may happen that you love a thing which is bad for you. Allah knows, and you know not'* - Quran 2:216. And also know that patience is rewarded with Heaven; *'peace be upon you, because you persevered in patience! Excellent indeed is the final home (Paradise)!'* - Quran 13:24.

Day
297

Note a positive moment of the last 24 hours

Write down one positive thing that has happened to you in the last 24 hours. It may be the narrow escape from a car accident you were about to be involved in? Go into as much detail as you can – what happened and how you escaped – so your brain recreates the moment and brings back those happy feelings you had. Re-read what you write throughout the day for an instant boost. Also, please Allah by thanking Him for this moment of happiness and, *insha'Allah* (Allah willing), you will have another moment tomorrow; *'...if you are grateful, I will certainly grant you more [favours]...'* - Quran 14:7.

Day
298

Be amazed by plant life

Watch a documentary on plant life. These are readily available online. Despite seeming to be very still, you will be amazed at how plants live and die just like mankind and animals. They too, fight amongst each other, compete for mates, reproduce, distribute themselves in new territories and form alliances with certain creatures, but the drama is a lot slower than ours. Witnessing the lives of plants will astound you, broaden your senses of enjoyment to life outside of yours, and put your daily worries into perspective. But above all, realise the magnificence of Allah and that surely, for His creations, He should be glorified day and night just like those very plants glorify Him. *'And in the Earth are neighbouring tracts of land, orchards of grapes, plantations and date palms, some of which grow in clusters whilst others do not: watered with the same water, yet some of them We make more excellent than others to eat. Behold, verily in these things there are signs for those who understand!'* - Quran 13:4.

Day
299

Reminisce over fun times of the past

Dig out some old photos and reminisce. Look back and smile at the fun times you had with your family and friends. Relive in detail the moments when you were 5 years old or 18 years old, the time you rode your first bike or went on your first holiday abroad. Enjoy reminiscing and say *alhamdulillah* (all praise and thanks be to Allah), for those happy moments and now these happy memories. More importantly, realise that one day, perhaps in 20 years' time, you will look back at photos you take and memories you make today and reminisce fondly about these days too. So make effort to cherish and be thankful for the present moments before they become just photos. *'And if you were to count the blessings of Allah, never will you be able to count them'* - Quran 14:34.

Day
300

Fully concentrate on your prayers

Today, challenge yourself to fully concentrate in your salah (five obligatory prayers). As you step onto your prayer mat and raise your hands back with *'Allahu akbar'*, throw behind all your worldly thoughts. Stop and focus on the conversation you are about to have with your Lord. Be sincere in this act of love and devote all of your mind, soul and body to nothing but your Creator, the Most Worthy. This is a profound form of spiritual escapism where nothing else in the world seems to matter, and in that bubble, it is just you and Your Lord. For your soul, this is true joy. *'Surely, in the remembrance of Allah do hearts find rest'* - Quran 13:28.

Day

301

Have a relaxing breakfast

Wake up early enough to have a relaxing breakfast. It is one of the most important meals of the day as your body needs fuel the most in the morning. Have something healthy – cereal, fruit, brown toast, a smoothie – something that will give you a good energy boost until lunchtime. Put away that technology and use this quiet time to also awaken yourself spiritually; perhaps pray a little, contemplate, read or enjoy simply staring out of the window at the new sky Allah has uncovered for you. *'And He has made everything in the Heavens and Earth of service to you. It is all from Him. These are certainly signs [of Allah's powers] for people who reflect'* - Quran 45:13.

Day
302

Accept the good & bad Allah decides for you

Accept everything in your life that Allah has decided for you. Your losses, your gains, your hopeful future, your difficult past. Know that; *'what hit you, could not have missed you and what missed you could not have hit you'*, as said by Prophet Muhammad (pbuh). Destiny is destiny, fate is fate. Know that nothing has happened, or nothing will happen, except what Allah meant it to be. No human being or thing can change your blessings or hardships. Only lawful du'aa can make changes to what is already written; *'du'aa is the most potent weapon of a believer, it can change fate while no action of ours ever can'* - Prophet Muhammad (pbuh). Therefore, profusely make du'aa that Allah does what is best for you, and then without fear or regrets, rest your heart with Allah, be patient in bad times, be grateful in good times, and accept His decree as the most-wise and best decision for you. Allah is the Most-wise, He makes the best decisions and His decision-making ability cannot be beaten, so trust Him. Acceptance of Allah's decisions, by being grateful or patient, is a key factor to inner contentment and true faith. *'Say: "Nothing shall ever happen to us except what Allah has ordained for us. He is our Mawla (protector)." And in Allah let the believers put their trust'* - Quran 9:51. You are exactly where Allah wants you to be, so accept your life; be patient, be grateful.

Day

303

Note all your achievements

Write a list of all your achievements. This could be your academic qualifications at university, your sporting achievements, your top performance at work, making your partner smile often, becoming a parent, learning how to cook the perfect steak last week, raising a large amount of money for charity recently. Think about how these achievements have enriched your life and the lives of others. Be thankful to Allah for giving you the ability to achieve. You will see that you are blessed and have a lot to feel proud of. *'And if you were to count the blessings of Allah, never will you be able to count them'* - Quran 14:34.

Day
304

Life's struggles will lead to Allah & Heaven

Realise today, that your life's struggles will eventually lead to you meeting Your Creator and His Paradise. Without doubt, life is difficult and can be hard work. Dealing with disappointments in failing dreams, unhappiness within yourself, illness, death of loved ones, troubles within your home and the imperfections of the world is tough. Allah understands this. He acknowledges it. And tells you to know that the struggles of living and the hard work in remaining patient will soon be repaid and you will finally meet Him and His Heaven. *'Oh mankind, indeed you are ever toiling towards your Lord, painfully toiling... But you shall meet Him'* - Quran 84:6. Hold onto that hope today.

Day
305

Help someone

Help someone today. Perhaps you could cook dinner for your elderly relative or neighbour, take someone grocery shopping, pick some flowers for your mother, take some food down to the local homeless shelter or send someone a nice message. Apart from the obvious recipient, the person who will benefit from your act of charity will be you, because; you will feel satisfied at seeing a positive change in yourself, you will have the pleasure of watching another smile as a result of your actions, you will find peace and solace in your heart at having done something good and there will also be reward from Allah. Caring about others will also take your attention away from caring about yourself and your problems. But above all of that, your Lord, the purpose of your being, will be pleased with you. '*...And do good (to others); surely Allah loves the doers of good*' - Quran 2:195.

Day
306

Take a drink with you & go outdoors

Go outdoors for half an hour today. Wind, rain or shine. Try and go to a natural environment such as the sea, a park, a river, the canal or in the woods. Take a coffee with you or a cold drink. Light deprivation will make you feel tired. But stepping outside into the daylight releases brain chemicals, serotonin and dopamine, which will clear your mind, boost your energy and improve your mood. Take this moment to close your eyes and listen to the birds. Or look and reflect on the great beauty of nature that Allah has gifted to you for nothing in return but His remembrance. *'Or who has made the Earth firm to live in; made rivers in its midst; set mountains on it, and has placed a barrier between the two seas? [Can there be another] god besides Allah?...'-* Quran 27:61.

Day
307

Ponder over the meaning of surah al-Fatiha

Learn and ponder over the translation of *surah al-Fatiha*, chapter 1 of the Quran. It is probably the chapter of the Quran that you recite the most, especially when performing salah, and therefore understanding what you are saying to Allah and feeling a deep connection to the words each time you pray will give new life to your spirituality and relationship with Allah. The strengthening of your bond with your Lord will strengthen the peace within your heart, *insha'Allah* (Allah willing). *'Surely, in the remembrance of Allah do hearts find rest'* - Quran 13:28.

Day
308

Do one thing that makes you happy

Do one thing today that makes you happy. It may be; going to a coffee shop and reading a chapter of a novel, going for a sunset stroll alone, having a lie-in, eating a whole bar of chocolate, sitting in a candlelit bath, meeting a good friend, or playing video games. Make today about you. Not forgetting to praise Allah for giving you this moment of pleasure, however small. '*...If you are grateful, I will certainly grant you more [favours]...*' - Quran 14:7.

Day
309

Learn about how birds fly

Today, spend some time learning about how birds fly. How do their wings work? What keeps them up in the air? What do they see? What happens if it's dark or windy? What is their process of landing? Do planes work the same way? Learning something new and interesting is important for happiness and faith. Novelty broadens your mind beyond the trivialities of daily life, keeps you away from boredom, creates joy when you marvel at life's miracles, and pleases Allah, as He commands us to seek knowledge and reflect. *'And say: My Lord increase me in knowledge'* - Quran 20:114; *'...these are certainly signs for people who reflect'* - Quran 45:13.

Day
310

Master your mind by thinking positively

Be the master of your mind today, by only allowing positive thoughts into it. Your problems may be real, but the thoughts around them can change to make your problems not so problematic. 2,000 years ago, the Greek philosopher, Epictetus, said that people are disturbed *'not by things, but by the views we take of them'*. You may not be able to control the things around you, but you can control your thoughts by making them focus on the positives. If it is cloudy outside, focus on the fact that the sun is still there giving some light. If you are struggling to pay bills, focus on the fact that you have a roof over your head for at least another day. If you are suffering from heartbreak, focus on the fact that at least your heart is not physically in pain. *'Certainly, with every hardship there is ease'* - Quran 94:5.

Day

311

Imagine you have just gained eyesight

When you wake up, imagine you have been blind for all your life. Keep that thought in your head. Open your eyes. You can see. Be amazed at everything as though you are seeing things for the first time. Look at the colour of your hands, the sky above with the moving clouds, the dazzling rays of the sun, the gracefully flying birds, other people and their varying appearances, their fascinating actions. Watch them. Watch everything. You can see. Many cannot. *Alhamdulillah* (all praise and thanks be to Allah). *'So take what I have given you and be of the grateful ones'* - Quran 7:144.

Day
312

Take a gratitude pebble or shell

Go to the beach or a park today, and pick up a shell or a pebble. A small one to fit in your pocket or handbag. This will be your gratitude reminder. Every time you now see this, think of something you are currently grateful to Allah for, and smile. *'So take what I have given you and be of the grateful ones'* - Quran 7:144.

Day
313

Make du'aa instead of worrying

If you want something today, as a believer, the first thing you can do, is raise your hands before Allah and ask Him; the Giver of everything. If you have time to worry, you certainly have time to make du'aa. Allah says; '...indeed I am near. I answer the prayer of every caller (silent or audible) when he calls upon Me ...' - Quran 2:186. Your whole life can change with the power of du'aa; 'du'aa is the most potent weapon of a believer, it can change fate while no action of ours ever can' - Prophet Muhammad (pbuh). Do you want your project at work to be completed today? Want to be able to concentrate on your revision? Have an enjoyable time at the in-laws tonight? Big or small, whenever you want it, pause, raise your hands, ask Allah for it sincerely, ask that He ultimately does what is best for you in this matter, and have complete belief that only He can give you what you want, as nothing is impossible for Him; 'when He wills anything, His only command is to say "Be!" – and it is' - Quran 36:82. Allah guarantees to respond, one way or another. If He wills, He will give you what you want immediately, otherwise He will respond another time in another positive form or He will respond in Heaven – whatever He thinks is best for you. And above all that, Allah will love you and reward you just for asking; 'there is nothing more dear to Allah, than a servant making du'aa to Him' - Prophet Muhammad (pbuh).

Day
314

Note 3 things you are grateful for today

Think about 3 things you are grateful for today. Finishing work early? Being in a time where we have the internet and mobile phones? Having a mosque so near you? Write them down on a piece of paper. Re-read and savour these 3 things throughout your day, and each time you do, show gratitude firstly to Allah, and then to those people who play a part in these blessings. Grateful people are happier people, and less prone to stress and depression. Also in Islam, half of inner happiness is to be grateful in good times, an act for which you will also be greatly rewarded by Allah. *'Therefore remember Me. I will remember you. And be grateful to Me and do not be ungrateful'* - Quran 2:152.

Day
315

Plan your day

Plan your day. A person who plans their day has a more productive day, and productivity increases happiness. Write down all the things you want doing today. Balance the list with worship, work and life – just like Prophet Muhammad (pbuh) used to carefully do. Allocate time for prayers, job matters, chores and spending time with family, exercising, and even one of your hobbies. Now work through that list and make sure each one has a tick next to it by the end of the night. Knowing that you have had a balanced day will, *insha'Allah* (Allah willing), make you feel satisfied and content with yourself.

Day
316

Let Heaven influence your actions

Let your desire for Heaven influence your actions today. If you lead a good life, then Heaven is where you will live for eternity. A place where there is endless happiness. A place where you can have everything that you wish for. A place where no one will die. There will be no sadness, no anger, no ill feelings. Work for it, today, by simply doing things that you know will please Allah – prayers, gratitude, patience, being nice to others, giving to charity, refraining from sinful acts. Look forward to Heaven and let this be the reason for you to smile today. *'So give good news, to those who have faith and do good acts, that for them shall be gardens beneath which rivers flow...'* - Quran 2:25.

Day
317

Put Allah at the forefront of your mind

Put Allah at the forefront of your mind today. Your purpose in life is to worship, remember, please and love Allah. *'I have not created jinn and mankind (for any purpose) except to worship Me'* - Quran 51:56. Get into the habit of thinking about Him all the time. See the shining sun? Praise Allah. Feel a headache coming on? Ask Allah to give you ease. Enjoying a sandwich? Thank Allah for giving you this. Having a hard time with bills? Tell Allah you trust Him. Feeling happy when you see your child? Tell Allah you love Him for your blessings. Bringing Allah into your life will bring unwavering peace into your soul. *'Surely, in the remembrance of Allah do hearts find rest'*- Quran 13:28.

Day
318

Your wealth has already been set by Allah

Do not worry about money today because your wealth has already been written by Allah. We spend most of our time and energy chasing and worrying about money, yet it is paramount to understand that your allotted wealth in life had already been set by Allah before you were born, just like the date of your death. Nothing you do can increase it or decrease it. So work for your provision in a halal manner, because Allah commands you to work, but do not give your soul to chasing and stressing over money, whilst forgetting that the reason why you are commanded to work in the first place is to sustain yourself so you are able to fulfil your life's purpose of worshipping Allah (through prayers, spending time with your family, giving to charity, and so on). Know that, no matter how much extra time you spend at work when you should be pleasing Allah, how much you stress or how much you partake in illegal money-making acts, the specific amount that is written for you will come to you, regardless. *'If the son of Adam ran away from his provision as he runs away from death, then his provision would find him just as death finds him'* - Prophet Muhammad (pbuh). Simply make du'aa to Allah that He puts blessing and barakah in your wealth and focus on the important things today.

Day
319

Exercise for a physical & mental boost

Give yourself a physical and mental energy boost this morning by doing some exercise in your house (or you could do your own preferred workout). Stretch first. Then do 50 star jumps, 100 runs up and down the stairs and 50 star jumps again. Repeat if you can. You should be sweating by the end of it and raring to take the day on. Scientific research states that exercise is one of the most important factors in making us feel happy. Certain chemicals, like endorphins, increase drastically after a workout, which results in giving you a happy feeling. And generally, people who exercise are healthier, look trimmer, think more clearly and sleep better. Prophet Muhammad (pbuh) also advised us to look after our bodies, which are a gift from Allah, by implementing exercise into our lives. *'Then which of your Lord's favours will you deny?'* - Quran 55:13.

Day
320

Surround yourself with good & happy people

Surround yourself with good and happy people today. It is easy to begin to think negatively when you spend time with people who backbite about colleagues, are ungrateful for the blessings they have, constantly complain about life, use hateful speech towards others, and involve themselves in dark acts. On the other hand, if you are around people who are pious, kind to others, grateful for what they have and express happiness often, their goodness will rub onto you – and such friendship is one of life's greatest joys. Follow Prophet Muhammad's (pbuh) advice and carefully choose who you spend time with; *'a person is on the religion of his companions. Therefore let every one of you carefully consider the company he keeps'*. The best friends being; *'one whose appearance reminds you of God, and whose speech increases you in knowledge, and whose actions remind you of the Hereafter'*.

Day
321

Do something to better yourself

Repel boredom by doing something to better yourself. The feeling of boredom will make you feel unhappy. Read a book, listen to a useful talk online, clean up the house, learn a new art, offer to take your mother shopping, ask your elderly neighbour if he needs any help. All these activities are indirect worship of Allah, because Allah commands us to seek knowledge; *'and say: "My Lord! Increase me in knowledge"'*- Quran, 20:114, and to do good; *'"...and do good (to others); surely Allah loves the doers of good"'* - Quran 2:195. So the benefits of these activities will stay with you beyond the grave and at the same time, they will prevent you from being bored and feeling unhappy.

Day
322

Believe that Allah's decisions are the best

For every difficulty that you are currently going through, believe that Allah's decisions are the best. Whether you are going through a tough time at home, have lost someone to death, are sick or have just been burgled, remind yourself that this is Allah's decision – Allah is the Most-wise, He makes the best decisions and His decision-making ability cannot be beaten. So ask Him to do what is best for you in this matter, and trust Him. And know that whatever situation you are in right now, and whatever are Allah's reasons behind it, it is ultimately for the best, as you have the perfect opportunity to exhibit patience in Allah (by maintaining firm trust in your Lord's decision and continuing to please Him) which will earn you Heaven as a grand reward, *insha'Allah* (Allah willing). *'I have rewarded them this day for their patience and faithfulness: they are indeed the ones that have achieved bliss...'* - Quran 23:111.

Day
323

Go kick a ball in the park

Pick up your kids, your nephews, your friend's kids or maybe just an adult friend and go kick a ball in the park for a little while. Don't let poor weather stop you. Light deprivation will make you feel tired. But stepping outside into the daylight releases brain chemicals, serotonin and dopamine, which will clear your mind, boost your energy and improve your mood. Also, some exercise will increase the release of endorphins in your body, which will result in giving you a happy feeling. So getting outdoors, exercising and having some light-hearted fun is a triple ingredient recipe for a boost of happiness, *insha'Allah* (Allah willing). *'And if you were to count the blessings of Allah, never will you be able to count them'* - Quran 14:34.

Day
324

Note a positive moment of the last 24 hours

Write down one positive thing that has happened to you in the last 24 hours. It might be that email you received from an old friend? Go into as much detail as you can – what the email said and what memories it brought back – so your brain recreates the moment and brings back those happy feelings you had. Re-read what you write throughout the day for an instant boost. Also, please Allah by thanking Him for this moment of happiness and, *insha'Allah* (Allah willing), you will have another moment tomorrow; *'...if you are grateful, I will certainly grant you more [favours]...'* - Quran 14:7.

Day
325

Carry prayer beads with you

Carry a tasbee (prayer beads) with you everywhere today. In the car, at your desk, whilst shopping and when cooking. Use it to simply remember Allah. Say *Allahu akbar* (Allah is the Greatest), *Subhana'Allah* (glory be to Allah) or *Alhamdulillah* (all praise and thanks be to Allah). For your soul, this is true joy. And the feelings of peace and comfort will follow. *'Surely, in the remembrance of Allah do hearts find rest'* - Quran 13:28.

Day
326

Imagine you are lying in your cold grave

In the morning, before you get up from bed, spend 10 minutes lying there, with your eyes closed. Imagine you are in your cold grave. You have left behind your father, your sister, your sons, your wife, your best friend, your job, your 3 bedroomed house with the mortgage, your clothes, your Mercedes, your bank account with your savings. Life has passed and you are all alone. Death is inevitable. It is coming. Remember death. As it will ensure that you worry less about your daily issues, love more, fight less, and more importantly, it will inspire you to fill every minute of your day building on your love for Allah and for that Eternal Life After. *'The one who remembers death most often and the one who is well-prepared to meet it; these are the wise; honorable in this life and dignified in the Hereafter'* - Prophet Muhammad (pbuh).

Day
327

Start saving money every week

Save some money, even if it is a little, every week. This is a very simple concept but could make a big difference to your life. Your stresses would be significantly reduced if you had an emergency fund, so that, should the need arise for unexpected events, you have the required money and will not need to go down the road of debt. Saving is Islamically recommended so long as the appropriate zakat (charity) is given at the end of the year. Start today, and ask Allah to put blessings and barakah into your savings; *'call upon Me; I will respond to you'* - Quran 40:60.

Day
328

Write 3 things you are grateful for today

Think about 3 things you are grateful for today. Not being ill and in hospital? Being able to walk the streets without fearing your safety? Having the ability to love your Lord? Write them down on a piece of paper. Re-read and savour these 3 things throughout your day, and each time you do, show gratitude firstly to Allah, and then to those people who play a part in these blessings. Grateful people are happier people, and less prone to stress and depression. Also in Islam, half of inner happiness is to be grateful in good times, an act for which you will also be greatly rewarded by Allah. *'Therefore remember Me. I will remember you. And be grateful to Me and do not be ungrateful'* - Quran 2:152.

Day
329

Gather your family & read out a hadith

In the evening, gather your family around and read out a hadith (report of the sayings and actions of Prophet Muhammad (pbuh)) – which you can get online or from bookshops. It is said that when such a gathering occurs in a home for the purpose of gaining Islamic knowledge, the light of faith and peace penetrates each heart, angels join and pile to the sky to repent on the gatherer's behalf, and corruption in your household will disappear. Above this, you will learn about Islam, thus reminding yourself of the sole purpose of your life. *'I have not created jinn and mankind (for any purpose) except to worship Me'* - Quran 51:56; *'and say: My Lord increase me in knowledge'* - Quran 20:114.

Day
330

Give the world your gift of prayer

Today, you can give the greatest gift to everyone in this world – dead, alive, and yet to be born. The gift of a prayer. '...*Indeed I am near. I answer the prayer of every caller (silent or audible) when he calls upon Me ...*' - Quran 2:186. Your prayer is the most powerful asset you possess. You can change lives with it; '*du'aa is the most potent weapon of a believer, it can change fate while no action of ours ever can*' - Prophet Muhammad (pbuh). Take 10 minutes out today to kneel down, raise your hands in the direction of the Kaba and sincerely ask Allah for the happiness of everyone in the world. Mention your family, friends and neighbours by their names, know their desires and make specific prayers for them. Think of the hungry in the world and pray for their ease. Think of the depressed in the world and pray for their contentment. Think of the orphans in the world and pray for their salvation. Think of the faithless in the world and pray that they be guided to the path of light. Not only are you helping others but you're also helping yourself, as your prayers for others will return to you; '*the supplication of a Muslim for his brother in his absence will certainly be answered. Every time he makes a supplication for good for his brother, the angel appointed for this particular task says: "Ameen! May it be for you, too"*' - Prophet Muhammad (pbuh).

Day

331

Be clean at all times

Be clean at all times. Shower in the morning, exfoliate, scrub, wax, brush, floss, perfume yourself, wear clean and ironed clothes, and wash throughout the day with every visit to the bathroom. Generally, as a human, you will find being fresh and clean pleasing and re-energising. But at the same time, as a Muslim, it is an important act of worship to Allah to be clean at all times, as this is a command of His. *'Truly, Allah loves those who turn to Him in repentance and loves those who purify themselves'* - Quran 2:222.

Day
332

Have a snack somewhere nice outdoors

Have breakfast, lunch or an after-work dessert somewhere nice outdoors. Drive to the beach, or any other natural setting, like a lake, river or mountain. Light deprivation will make you feel tired. But stepping outside into the daylight releases brain chemicals, serotonin and dopamine, which will clear your mind, boost your energy and improve your mood. If it is too cold to be sitting outside, stay in your car but still enjoy the scenery. Savour the peaceful moment and reflect on the Earth that Allah has created for you. '...*And they think deeply about the creation of the Heavens and the Earth, [saying] "Our Lord! You did not create (all) of this without a purpose, glory be to You"...*' - Quran 3:191.

Day
333

Believe you'll have what you want in Heaven

Write down 5 things that you dream to have and truly believe that you will have them in Heaven. Do you desire; unconditional love? To meet your Creator? To fly like a bird? A constant state of happiness? Unlimited friends? A palace made of crystals? '... *In Heaven, there will be whatever the heart desires, whatever pleases the eye ...*' - Quran 43:71. Ask Allah for them; '...*indeed I am near. I answer the prayer of every caller (silent or audible) when he calls upon Me ...*' - Quran 2:186, and one day you will have them, *insha'Allah* (Allah willing). Let this be the reason for you to smile today.

Day
334

Write 'A' on your hand for Alhamdulillah

Get a pen and write an 'A' on the back of your hand. 'A' for *Alhamdulillah* (all praise and thanks be to Allah). Every time you see that 'A', look around you for something that you have been gifted with by Allah. This could be a good nights sleep, a hot cup of tea, a delicious burrito for lunch, an easy day at work or the sight of your mother's glowing face. Each time, smile and say *alhamdulillah*. Grateful people are happier people, and less prone to stress and depression. And according to Islam, half of inner happiness is to be grateful in good times. Gratitude will also gain you Allah's pleasure. *'…If you are grateful, I will certainly grant you more [favours]…'* - Quran 14:7.

Day
335

Note a positive moment of the last day

Write down one positive thing that has happened to you in the last 24 hours. It might be that comforting hug that your mother gave you? Go into as much detail as you can – why she hugged you and how you felt – so your brain recreates the moment and brings back those happy feelings you had. Re-read what you write throughout the day for an instant boost. Also, please Allah by thanking Him for this moment of happiness, and *insha'Allah* (Allah willing), you will have another moment tomorrow; *'…if you are grateful, I will certainly grant you more [favours]…'* - Quran 14:7.

Day
336

Look at your successes of the last 5 years

Look back at your successes in the last 5 years. Write down as many as you can think of. Did you get a new job? Did you pass your exams? Did you get married and complete half your deen? Did you give birth to a beautiful baby? Did you take part in a charity event? Did you go for hajj or umrah? Did you make a new friend? Did you start praying your 5 daily prayers? Did you learn how to swim? Did you read the Quran in English? Did you overcome your fear of flying? You will recognise how accomplished and blessed you have actually been. *Alhamdulillah* (all praise and thanks be to Allah). Imagine what successes the next 5 years could hold? – *insha'Allah* (Allah willing). *'And if you were to count the blessings of Allah, never will you be able to count them'* - Quran 14:34.

Day
337

Pick a room & have a clear out

Pick a room and have a clear out. Get rid of clutter, things you have not used in a year, or don't need. Shoes, paperwork, clothes, books, toys, tools, furniture. Give it away to charity or throw it away. Be ruthless. You will not miss this extra baggage. Don't feel that you might need it one day, live for today and trust in Allah for tomorrow. Getting rid of your attachment to material possessions will take away the physical disorder in your life to make room for calmness, freedom and clarity of thinking; help the people you donate to; and lead you to living a simple, non-extravagant life as Islam advises. *'The son of Adam will not pass away from Allah until he is asked about five things…'*, the fourth being; *'how did he spend his wealth…'* - Prophet Muhammad (pbuh). Our excess wealth is only there to test us – use it for doing good, and from now on, try to only buy what you need. *'…The righteous is the one who…gives wealth, in spite of love for it, to relatives, orphans, the needy…'* - Quran 2:177.

Day
338

Make people happy by being kind

Make people happy today. Say something nice to your partner, give way to a driver at a junction, send a pleasant message to a friend, offer to make your colleague a hot drink, open the door for a stranger, greet someone with the Islamic greeting; *assalamu'alaikum warahmatullahi wabarakatuh* (may the peace, mercy, and blessings of Allah be with you), take your kids out for ice cream. This selfless kindness will, by nature, make the recipient happy, make you happy, and most importantly, make Allah happy – which helps fulfil your life's purpose of worshipping Him. *'Is there any reward for good, other than good?'* - Quran 55:60.

Day
339

Bad moments are good for your afterlife

If you are feeling down today, wondering why 'bad things happen to good people', realise that 'bad' things do not happen to good people. Allah tells us that we will all be tested; *'most definitely We will test you with some fear and hunger, some loss in goods, lives and the fruits (of your toil)…'*- Quran 2:155. Even His most beloved, Prophet Muhammad (pbuh), was tested with hardships, more than you ever will be. But sometimes Allah puts you through the hard times because He knows that it is when you are at your lowest that you are most likely to; find Him, turn to Him for comfort, realise your purpose in life, know that only Allah is the Giver and Taker, and then submit and be patient with whatever He has willed for you, and perhaps afterwards, be grateful to Him when He makes life better. All these attributes will then ultimately result in you earning a place in Heaven, *insha'Allah* (Allah willing). *'…But give good news to those who patiently persevere. Those who, when any difficulty befalls them, say: 'Surely, to Allah we belong and to Him we shall return. Those are the ones upon whom are blessings and mercy from their Lord and it is those who are rightly guided'* - Quran 2:155-157. Those seemingly 'bad' things you experience in this life, are actually good things for your afterlife. *'…He will give you [something] better than what was taken from you…'* - Quran 8:70. And remember; *'Allah does not burden a soul more than it can bear'* - Quran 2:286.

Day
340

Set a new goal for yourself

Today, set a goal for yourself that you would want to achieve in the next year. Perhaps it is to learn a new art, play in a football team, write a book, learn about the history of Islam. Buy the equipment, make applications, put pen to paper, borrow a history book. Whatever it is, start working on it today. Working towards something new and interesting plays a key role in happiness; it broadens your mind, keeps you away from boredom and creates self-satisfaction within. *'And if you were to count the blessings of Allah, never will you be able to count them'* - Quran 14:34.

Day
341

Do some exercise

Give yourself a physical and mental energy boost this morning by doing some exercise. You can do these in your bedroom (or you could do your own preferred workout). Stretch first. Then do 100 sit ups, 100 push ups, 100 squats. Repeat if you can. You should be sweating by the end of it and raring to take the day on. Scientific research states that exercise is one of the most important factors in making us feel happy. Certain chemicals, like endorphins, increase drastically after a workout, which results in giving you a happy feeling. And generally, people who exercise are healthier, look trimmer, think more clearly and sleep better. Prophet Muhammad (pbuh) also advised us to look after our bodies, which are a gift from Allah, by implementing exercise into our lives. *'Then which of your Lord's favours will you deny?'* - Quran 55:13.

Day
342

Accept what Allah has decreed for you

Accept what Allah has decreed for you. Allah is the Most-wise, He makes the best decisions and His decision-making ability cannot be beaten, so ask Him to do what is best for you and trust Him. And know that whatever situation you are in right now, and whatever are Allah's reasons behind it, it is ultimately for the best. Whether you have just bought a yacht or have just lost your house, it is for the best. As you have the perfect opportunity to exhibit either patience in Allah (by maintaining firm trust in your Lord's decision and continuing to please Him) or gratitude to Allah (by thanking Him and continuing to please Him); both of which will open up the doors of Heaven as a reward, *insha'Allah* (Allah willing). *'...And it may be that you dislike a thing which is good for you and that you like a thing which is bad for you. Allah knows but you do not know'* - Quran 2:216; *'...if he (the believer) is granted ease of living, he is thankful; and this is best for him. And if he is afflicted with a hardship, he perseveres; and this is best for him'* - Prophet Muhammad (pbuh). Acceptance of Allah's decree, by being grateful or patient, is a key factor to inner contentment and true faith. You are exactly where Allah wants you to be, so accept your life; be patient, be grateful.

Day
343

Make your day revolve around Allah

Today, make effort to ensure your day revolves around Allah, by carrying out your tasks in His name and for His pleasure. From the moment we open our eyes in the morning, we tend to get caught up with the activities of the day; breakfast, work, meeting with friends or family, grocery shopping, dinner preparations, winding down for bed, that we forget the sole purpose of our life – to know, to worship and to love our Creator – Allah. *'I have not created jinn and mankind (for any purpose) except to worship Me'* - Quran 51:56. That is your purpose and everything you do should be for Allah's love. So continue with your day but do your tasks in Allah's name and make Allah's pleasure your motivation. *'Say, "Indeed, my prayer, my acts of worship, my life and my death are for Allah, Lord of the worlds"'* - Quran 6:162.

Day
344

Zoom in on a blessing currently in your life

Focus on one good blessing currently in your life. It could be the love your family gives you, the peace inside your home, your beautiful children, your good health, your stable job, your loyal partner, your book collection. Zoom in on this particular blessing of yours today. Think about it often – how it makes you feel, the past enjoyment it has given you, and the times you still have to enjoy it. Grateful people are happier people, and less prone to stress and depression. Also in Islam, half of inner happiness is to be grateful in good times, an act for which you will also be greatly rewarded by Allah. '...*And Allah will soon reward the grateful ones*' - Quran 3:144.

Day
345

Make yourself smile all day

Make yourself smile all day, even if you don't feel like it. A smiling person draws others and is thought to be more attractive, pleasant, sincere, competent and sociable than the one who does not. By physically smiling, you are releasing positive energy and thoughts, not only to those who see you, but to yourself too, which in turn will make you all feel good. On top of this, Allah will also be pleased. *'Do not think little of any good deed, even if it is just greeting your brother with a cheerful smile'* and; *'to smile in the face of your brother is charity given on your behalf'* - Prophet Muhammad (pbuh).

Day
346

Notice the big & fascinating world

Lift your head up and notice the big and fascinating world around you. Marvel at the vast sky when you walk, the quirky behaviours of your acquaintances, the squirrels playing in the trees, the twinkle in your child's eyes when she smiles, the richness in colour of the fruit you bite into, the gentleness of your breathing despite the buzz around you, the cool breeze of the wind on your face. Stop dwelling on insignificant issues in your life and open yourself up to let in the simple, yet fascinating wonders that Allah has placed right in front of you at every moment. Reflect. *'…And they think deeply about the creation of the Heavens and the Earth, [saying] "Our Lord! You did not create (all) of this without a purpose, glory be to You"…'* - Quran 3:191.

Day
347

Replace a boring task with a treat

Find a boring task you have for today and replace it with treat-time for yourself. Some more emails to send? Send them tomorrow morning. Ironing? It can wait another day. Cooking tonight? Make something simple or get a takeout. Use this extra time you have saved to do something you love. Read. Sit in the bath. Get a dessert. Go for a walk. Visit your parents. Play a game. These are the simplest of blessings that Allah can bestow into your day. Say *alhamdulillah* (all praise and thanks be to Allah). *'Then which of your Lord's favours will you deny?'* - Quran 55:13.

Day
348

Sleep for 8 hours tonight

Sleep for 8 hours tonight. Be firm with this – get ready for bed early. Sleep is absolutely essential for happiness. It allows you to function well the next day, be in a good mood and have the required energy to work, socialise and pray. Studies suggest that an extra hour of sleep a day would do more for a person's happiness than a $60,000 raise in annual salary. Allah has gifted you with sleep for your serenity. Accept His blessing with open arms and by doing so you are turning sleep into a form of worship to Allah. *'And remember when He made slumber fall upon you as a means of serenity from Him'* - Quran 8:11.

Day
349

Sacrifice a buy & give the money to charity

Give a little bit of your money to charity today. Forgo that pair of shoes you wanted to buy or that special dinner you were going to have. Go online, find a charity where the poor are struggling to have clean water or dying of starvation and make an online donation – be it £1 or $100; whatever you can afford. And when you click 'donate', close your eyes and imagine the smile on the face of that little boy, girl, or mother, as though you are handing them a much needed loaf of bread or warm blanket. The beneficiary will be pleased, you will be pleased, and above all, your Lord will be pleased. '...And do good (to others); surely Allah loves the doers of good' - Quran 2:195, '...The righteous is the one who...gives wealth, in spite of love for it, to relatives, orphans, the needy...' - Quran 2:177.

Day
350

Savour all you touch, see, hear & taste

Savour and appreciate everything you touch, see, hear and taste today with an *alhamdulillah* (all praise and thanks be to Allah). Your daughter's laughter, the blossomed tree outside your house, the sweet peach you bite into, your living mother, the rain on your face, the warmth of your husband's hand in yours, the soft pillow you rest your cheek on. Prophet Muhammad (pbuh) continually reminded people to be grateful to their Lord. Grateful people are happier people, and less prone to stress and depression. Also in Islam, half of inner happiness is to be grateful in good times, an act for which you will also be greatly rewarded by Allah. '...*And Allah will soon reward the grateful ones*' - Quran 3:144.

Day
351

Vow to only think & speak positive

Put your hand on your heart and vow today to only think and speak positive. If it is too cold, do not complain; think that it could be colder. When you are hungry, be glad that you will be able to eat at some point in the day. If you are feeling depressed, be thankful that you are physically healthy and safe. When you get angry with your wife, note that anger is sinful and pointless, and instead try to remember her many good points. Actively refuse to think or speak anything negative, and positivity will seep into you. *'And speak good to people'* - Quran 2:83. And also, be aware that each time you complain, you are complaining about Allah's decisions and therefore complaining against Allah Himself. This would be hugely disrespectful and ungrateful of you, because Allah is your Creator and no matter what your circumstances are, you started off life with nothing and have therefore been blessed with a lot. *'And if you were to count the blessings of Allah, never will you be able to count them'* - Quran 14:34.

Day
352

Fresh air is a must today

Fresh air is a must today. Sometimes, all you need is air. Rain, wind or shine, take a 30 minute walk outside. Walking will trigger your body's relaxation responses, clear your mind and help reduce stress. Try and go when it is light, as light deprivation can make you feel tired. But stepping outside into the daylight releases brain chemicals, serotonin and dopamine, which will recharge your mind, boost your energy and improve your mood. Feel the fresh air kiss your face, stare up at the sky, look around and marvel at Allah's creations. '...*"Our Lord! You did not create (all) of this without a purpose, glory be to You"*...' - Quran 3:191.

Day
353

Focus on the purpose of your life

Focus on your purpose today and you will feel contented. It is a fact that people who have a sense of purpose and meaning in life tend to be happier people. As a Muslim, you have only one purpose in life, and that is to love Allah; *'I have not created jinn and mankind (for any purpose) except to worship Me'* - Quran 51:56. Allah created food so you will have energy in the day to worship Him with prayer and do good deeds that please Him. You are made to work in order to sustain yourself and your family enough to be able to carry out your acts of worship. He instils sleep in your life to rejuvenate you for the next day's service to Him. You have family and friends to give you an opportunity to please Allah by being kind and loving towards them. And He surrounds you with natural beauty and gifts so that you may look up in awe and glorify Him. Everything you do or have today, should be to fulfil your purpose – to please, love and worship Allah. Focus on this and you will be more contented.

Day
354

Pick 3 things you like about your appearance

Look in the mirror and pick out 3 things that you like about your appearance. You will find at least 3 – the twinkle in your eyes, your white smile, your dimple, your long eye lashes, your thick hair, your slender figure. Now focus on those aspects every time you look at your reflection, and smile, disregarding everything else you may dislike. Grateful people are happier people, and less prone to stress and depression. *Alhamdulillah* – thank Allah for your small beauties. *'So take what I have given you and be of the grateful ones'* - Quran 7:144.

Day
355

You are one of the lucky ones on this planet

Realise that you are one of the lucky ones on this planet. There are approximately 1 billion people living worldwide on less than $1 a day. 2.6 billion living on less than $2 a day (study by the United Nations Development Program 2007). And, centuries ago, the situation was a lot worse than this for the majority of the world. Deeply carry this thought with you throughout the day and realise that you are one of the fortunate ones. Allah could have very easily placed you in one of the poorer parts of the world, and still can. Be genuinely grateful and cherish all the blessings you have been given; *'...if you are grateful, I will certainly grant you more [favours]...'* - Quran 14:7.

Day
356

Think of Allah the most

Today, make Allah the one you think about most. *'Laa illaha illallah'* means *'there is no diety worthy of worship except Allah'*. What do you think of the most, and therefore; what is your heart most attached to, what makes you most happy and most sad, what do you rely on most, what would break you if it disappeared? If, throughout the day, you find yourself thinking about your partner, your house renovations or your friends more than you are thinking of your Lord, then, practically, you are making these things your *illah* (the object of your worship). That must change immediately to be a true believer, as our bodies, our hearts belong to Allah and we were created only to worship Him; *'I have not created jinn and mankind (for any purpose) except to worship Me'* - Quran 51:56. Not only that; Allah is the Greatest and Eternal, therefore make Him your *illah* and He will never disappoint you – unlike people and materials. So continue to love your partner, continue to work on your house and continue to have friends, but do it because these things please Allah. Make the pleasure of Allah your daily focus and motivation. Practically, what is your *illah*? Say Allah, prove that today and surely you will find peace. *'But those that truly believe, love Allah more than anything else...'* - Quran 2:165.

Day
357

Read a poem

Read a poem today. Search online for spiritual poems relating to God such as Rumi's 'A Moment of Happiness'. Or you could try other types of poems written by William H Davies, Maya Angelou or William Shakespeare. Words are one of the greatest forms of expression and reading a poem can bring joy and awaken a part of your mind that perhaps otherwise, lies sleeping. And above that, you may consider reading and learning about literature a form of worship to Allah, because Allah commands us to seek knowledge; *'and say: "My Lord! Increase me in knowledge"'* - Quran 20:114.

Day
358

Rid dark thoughts & feelings before you sleep

As you rest your head on your pillow tonight, make effort to rid all dark thoughts and feelings from your heart and mind. Forgive and apologise to the person you may have argued with today. Block out the worries you have – leave those for another day. Turn your night into a night of worship by sleeping in the name of Allah and with the intention of resting so you may serve Him tomorrow. And as you finally close your eyes, think about the peace you will feel in Heaven and smile. *'They will not hear therein ill or sinful speech. But only the saying of: Peace! Peace!'* - Quran 56:25-26.

Day
359

Learn about insects

Spend an hour or so today learning about the bodily functions of insects. Do they have a pulse? Do they breathe in oxygen? How do they mate? Do they have feelings and thoughts? Do they grieve? Learning something new and interesting is important for happiness and faith. Novelty broadens your mind beyond the trivialities of daily life, keeps you away from boredom, creates joy when you marvel at life's miracles, and pleases Allah, as He commands us to seek knowledge and reflect. *'And say: My Lord increase me in knowledge'* - Quran - 20:114; *'...these are certainly signs for people who reflect'* - Quran 45:13.

Day
360

Notice Allah's signs throughout your day

Notice Allah's signs as you go through your day. Every single thing that you experience today – the words your partner says to you in the morning, getting soaked in the rain on your way to work, the delicious pie you have for lunch, the lady at the bank who you have a conversation with, the laughter that escapes the lips of your friend, the unconditional love you see in your mother's eyes, your evening prayers, the respite you get when you lay to sleep tonight – all of it, has been put in your day for only one reason. And that is to show you and remind you of Allah. *'Verily! In the creation of the Heavens and the Earth, and in the alternation of night and day, there are indeed signs for those who have intelligence'* - Quran 3:190; *'..."Our Lord! You did not create (all) of this without a purpose, glory be to You"...'* - Quran 3:191. To show you the greatness, kindness and power of your Creator, so that you may come to love Him and fulfil your purpose; *'I have not created jinn and mankind (for any purpose) except to worship Me'* - Quran 51:56. Take a fresh, spiritual perspective of your life, by making note of your given signs today and telling yourself how they remind you of Allah.

Day
361

Note a positive moment of the last 24 hours

Write down one positive thing that has happened to you in the last 24 hours. It might be the party you organised for your son? Go into as much detail as you can – who came and how your son felt – so your brain recreates the moment and brings back those happy feelings you had. Re-read what you write throughout the day for an instant boost. Also, please Allah by thanking Him for this moment of happiness and, *insha'Allah* (Allah willing), you will have another moment tomorrow; *'...if you are grateful, I will certainly grant you more [favours]...'* - Quran 14:7.

Day
362

Live today like you won't be alive tomorrow

Live today as though you don't expect to be alive tomorrow. *'When the morning comes to you, then do not expect to see the evening, and when you see the night, do not expect to see the morning'* - Prophet Muhammad (pbuh). But that does not mean give up everything and sit on your prayer mat all day, crying. It simply means reminding yourself of your purpose in life – *'I have not created jinn and mankind (for any purpose) except to worship Me'* - Quran 51:56 – and turning your day into a day of worship to Allah, by continuing your normal lawful tasks, but doing them solely to please Allah. Go to work and make an honest living; Allah loves the righteous and commands us to work to sustain our lives of servitude. Eat a healthy breakfast, lunch and dinner; so that you have enough energy to do acts that please your Lord. Pray all your 5 prayers; Allah loves the submissive. Be nice and loving to all you meet; Allah loves the kind. Go see natural beauty and praise Allah; Allah loves the one who glorifies Him. Thank Allah when you have drank; Allah loves the grateful. Resist sin; Allah loves the good. Beg Allah to forgive you for your mistakes; Allah loves the one who repents. Raise your hands and ask Allah for whatever you wish for; Allah loves the one who asks. Throw out all your sadness, worries and fears, by being patient and trusting Allah completely, to eternally take care of you and all you love; Allah loves the one who is patient and trusts Him. Remember Allah at all times; Allah loves those that remember Him. So, if it actually is your last day, then you will not have wasted it away and done your best in fulfilling your purpose and earning a place in Heaven. Find peace in this.

Day
363

Write 3 things you are grateful for today

Think about 3 things you are grateful for today. Living so close to a beach or a park? Having the right to vote for your government? Not being in an abusive relationship? Write them down on a piece of paper. Re-read and savour these 3 things throughout your day, and each time you do, show gratitude firstly to Allah, and then to those people who play a part in these blessings. Grateful people are happier people, and less prone to stress and depression. Also in Islam, half of inner happiness is to be grateful in good times, an act for which you will also be greatly rewarded by Allah. *'...If you are grateful, I will certainly grant you more [favours]...'* - Quran 14:7.

Day
364

Ask Allah for good changes in your life

If you are wishing for change, ask Allah. *'There is no change and no strength except by Allah'.* What is it that you want? Ask Allah for it. Today. It is as simple as that. Allah reassures you; *'…indeed I am near. I answer the prayer of every caller (silent or audible) when he calls upon Me …'* - Quran 2:186. Your whole life can change with the power of du'aa; *'du'aa is the most potent weapon of a believer, it can change fate while no action of ours ever can'* - Prophet Muhammad (pbuh). Worried about your future? Ask Allah to make it easy. Searching for peace? Beg Allah to pour it into your heart. Wanting to get over the loss of a loved one? Plead with Allah. Raise your hands, ask Allah for it sincerely, ask that He ultimately does what is best for you in this matter, and have complete belief that only He can give you what you want, as nothing is impossible for Him; *'when He wills anything, His only command is to say "Be!" – and it is'*- Quran 36:82. Allah guarantees to respond, one way or another. If He wills, He will give you what you want immediately, otherwise He will respond another time in another positive form or He will respond in Heaven – whatever He thinks is best for you. And above all that, Allah will love you and reward you just for asking; *'there is nothing more dear to Allah, than a servant making du'aa to Him'* - Prophet Muhammad (pbuh).

Day
365

Visualise Heaven in detail

Think of the final destination; Heaven. Close your eyes and imagine yourself there. Be specific. Visualise: having more beauty than any woman or man on this planet; gliding through the grounds of your magnificent palace; being lost in the joyous embrace of your family and friends that had passed away, flying through the white skies of Paradise, catching shooting stars with your hands, kissing moons with your lips, swimming under waterfalls of honey and in seas of melted chocolate, being waited on by Angels who will bring you fruits, wines and cakes. And, not forgetting the most spell-binding moment; imagine yourself finally meeting Allah, the Greatest. Go as wild as you want with your imagination but even then Prophet Muhammad (pbuh) said that; *'Allah says: "I have prepared for My righteous slaves that which no eye has seen, no ear has heard and it has never crossed the mind of man."'* Ask Allah to make your daydreams come true – *'…indeed I am near. I answer the prayer of every caller (silent or audible) when he calls upon Me …'* - Quran 2:186 – and one day they will come true, and you will find eternal happiness, *insha'Allah* (Allah willing).

Start again from
Day
1

Also by Safiya Hussain

Three Thousand Miles for a Wish

Printed in Great Britain
by Amazon

27200744R00215